Mother Teresa

Always the Poor

José Luis González-Balado

**National Link of the
Co-Workers of Mother Teresa
in Spain**

LIGUORI
PUBLICATIONS

One Liguori Drive
Liguori, Missouri 63057
(314) 464-2500

Imprimi Potest:
Edmund T. Langton, C.SS.R.
Provincial, St. Louis Province
Redemptorist Fathers

Imprimatur:
+ John N. Wurm, S.T.D., Ph.D.
Vicar General, Archdiocese of St. Louis

ISBN Number 0-89243-134-2
Library of Congress Number 80-83484

This book has been adapted from the original Spanish
version entitled *Madre Teresa de los Pobres Más Pobres,*
published in Spain in the Catalonian language.

Cover design by Pam Hummelsheim

A Word of Thanks

For their many hours of help in preparing the English-language edition of this book, the author would like to express deep thanks to the following Co-Workers of Mother Teresa:

Mrs. Patricia Kump, National Link for the United States;

Mrs. Diane Hattery, Assistant Treasurer of the Co-Workers of Mother Teresa in America;

Eileen Egan, Consultant to the Co-Workers;

Janet Playfoot González, wife of the author and Co-Worker of Mother Teresa.

About the Author

In Western Europe, books from the pen of José Luis González-Balado have been translated into French, Italian, Catalonian, Portuguese, German, and English. His writings include popular studies of Pope John Paul II, Brazilian archbishop Dom Helder Camara, Brother Roger of Taizé, and Ernesto Cardenal. The author's familiarity with Mother Teresa and her work flows from his involvement and leadership among Spain's Co-Workers of Mother Teresa.

Contents

Words of Mother Teresa from Her Co-Worker Newsletters

My dear Co-Workers,

I know you will be delighted to know that our Sisters and Brothers keep growing in numbers and, I hope, in holiness also. Our number of houses are becoming more like a bridge of love and compassion, where the poor and the sick come face to face and so realize that they are brothers.

And this is where you, my Co-Workers, by your example, love and compassion, by your gentle touch, by your understanding love in your own home first and then in your next door neighbor, have lit a light and created in the world a concern, an awareness, a pressure of the poor, our brother, our sister.

Your simple acts of love and care keep that light burning. Never think that a small action done to your neighbor is not worth much. It is not how much we do that is pleasing to God, but how much love we put into the doing. That is what the good God looks for — because He is love and He has made us in His image to love and to be loved.

Make sure you know your neighbor, for that knowledge will lead you to great love and love to personal service.

Do not let money so preoccupy you as to forget that we and our people are more important to God than all the lilies of the field and the birds of the air. Therefore, try more and more to understand that yours is a way of life — the way of Jesus — that will lead you to the perfect love of God and your neighbors. That is holiness. For holiness is not the luxury of the few, but it is a simple duty for you and for me.

Bring this love, this holiness into your very life, your home, your neighborhood, your country and the whole world. For this we need to pray. Let every Co-Worker begin the family prayer. Help your neighbor to do the same. Through this prayer and sacrifice we will overcome the world.

Just as Jesus was the gift of God for the world, so we, each in our own way, have to be that love, that compassion of the Father for the world.

Jesus made Himself the Bread of Life to satisfy our hunger for God, our hunger for His love. But that was not enough for Him. He made Himself the hungry one, the naked one, the homeless one. And he said, "Whatever you do for the least of these my brothers, you do for me."

And today God loves the world so much that He gives you, He gives me, to love the world, to be His love, His compassion.

My prayer is with each of you — and I pray that each one of you will be holy, and so spread His love everywhere you go. Let His light of truth be in every person's life, so that God can continue loving the world through you and me.

1
"They Have Honored a Saint"

(**Paris Match,** *reporting the award of the*
1979 Nobel Peace Prize to Mother Teresa)

Only a handful of people throughout history have been canonized as saints by the Church.

Even fewer have been declared "living saints" in their lifetime.

Mother Teresa is one of these — a walking, living example of God's grace.

Mother Teresa invites comparison with Saint Francis in her humble devotion to the poorest of the poor — people who have forgotten how to smile; people who can no longer eat because they do not have the strength; people who can no longer cry because they have no tears.

Her life, like the lives of many saints, is filled with paradoxes and surprises.

When she won the 1979 Nobel Peace Prize, she asked that the traditional awards banquet not be held and that the money for it be donated to the poor.

Mother Teresa will not accept government grants, for that would entail a lot of bookkeeping, records, and equipment. She will not have endowments, fixed incomes, or security. She and Saint Francis agree.

Once she actually sent back a check for $500,000 because of a stipulation that the money was to be a security fund for her Missionaries of Charity. Since the very poor do not have security funds, neither would she. God would provide.

When Pope Paul VI gave Mother Teresa a limousine donated to him during a visit to India in 1964, she raffled off the car without so much as taking a ride in it. She then used the proceeds to build a colony for lepers in West Bengal.

Mother Teresa's reward? In the current ebb tide of institutional Christendom, one Catholic religious order that is flourishing rather than diminishing is her Congregation of the Missionaries of Charity.

"Why does all the world run after you?" Friar Masseo once asked Saint Francis.

Today the world seems to be running after Mother Teresa.

Just a few of the awards given her in addition to the Nobel Peace Prize include the John XXIII Peace Prize; the Albert Schweitzer International Prize; the Philippines' highest honor, the Magsaysay Award; the Father Hogan Emmaus Award for her work in defense of the unborn; the Jawaharlal Nehru Award of India; the Bharat Ratna (the Jewel of India), India's highest civilian award; and the Templeton Award for Progress in Religion.

Mother Teresa's picture appeared on the cover of *Time* for December 29, 1975. The accompanying article was entitled "Messengers of Love and Hope: LIVING SAINTS." *Time* said of Mother Teresa:

"Perhaps the best definition of sanctity may be one which is widely agreed upon; the saint is a window through which a different world is seen, a person through whom God's light shines. It is that light that many see in Mother Teresa. . . . Mother

Teresa is unique, even though many in the world affirm that they share her same faith."

Jean Vanier, also acclaimed by *Time* in this same issue on living saints, affirms: "Mother Teresa is a sign of the presence of Christ in the world in which we live."

Paris Match had Mother Teresa on its January 17, 1976, cover with the coverline: *There Are Still Saints Left.* In its story, it added further tribute: "To some, Mother Teresa is the most extraordinary woman of our century. In India, she is considered a national heroine. The most visible people in this world, from the Pope to the Queen of England, confide in her. But it is among the outcasts of this world where she is most at home."

Before going any further, I should point out that we must await the verdict of the Church before we canonize Mother Teresa as an actual saint. As a reporter, however, I can also add that this cynical world of ours seems to agree on one point at least: Mother Teresa is already being acclaimed a saint by popular opinion. There is something magnetic about her. People want to touch her, to be near her for a brief moment, to feel her presence.

Malcolm Muggeridge reports his feelings when he saw one old man bend his gray head down to kiss Mother Teresa's hand. "So they do to queens and eminences and great *seigneurs,*" writes the author in his book about Mother Teresa. "In this particular case, it was a gesture of perfect thankfulness to God — in which I shared — for helping our poor, stumbling minds and fearful hearts by showing us His everlasting truth in the guise of one homely face going about His work of love."

Journalists and writers around the world seem to vie with one another in praising Mother Teresa. In France, Raúl Follereau writes: "I see a heroine, a saint, in Mother Teresa. Her overwhelming popularity has not altered in the least her simplicity nor diminished her willingness for action. More than an example, Mother Teresa constitutes a symbol: the love without which nothing is possible."

In a German magazine, Arthur Beining writes: "Mother Teresa of Calcutta, Father Foucauld, and Archbishop Helder Camara can be included among the modern saints who will light up the future of the Church and the world."

An American newspaperman, Curtis Bill Pepper, has written: "Is Mother Teresa a saint? There are millions of people who say so. If asked why, they affirm that they *feel it*. If the questioning persists, they add: *Because her heart is as big as the world.*"

Such praise and the honors she has won have caused eyes to turn toward the light that Mother Teresa spreads like a lamp of love in our world of shadows.

2
From Albania to India at 18

"The road, you must follow it;
the pain, you must forget it;
the cup, you must drink it;
the pleasure, you must deny it,
and to the goal you must be committed."
Dag Hammarskjold

When Mother Teresa first went to Spain in 1976, she arrived on an Iberia Airline jumbo jet from New York very early in the morning. There were about a half-dozen people waiting for her at the airport. I was among them. Also present was a fan of Mother Teresa, an Iberia flight attendant who knew the ins and outs of the airline.

Juan Garcés, the flight attendant, was able to convince airline executives that the small, frail figure riding in the coach section was a sure candidate for the Nobel Peace Prize.

Spotting a chance for publicity, the Iberia management authorized the V.I.P. treatment for Mother Teresa. In the air, the pilot and the crew were alerted by radio and told to assist the nun in every way possible. So, to her complete surprise, Mother Teresa was ushered to a special first-class exit when the plane touched down and allowed to leave the plane before everyone else.

To spare her inconvenience and to free her for interviews, I offered to find Mother's luggage and clear it through customs. When I went to the luggage section, I received my first surprise. Along with the luxurious leather suitcases belonging to the jet setters, the conveyor belt brought a modest cloth bag with Mother Teresa's name on it. The contrast was startling.

My next surprise came when I took the small bag to the customs officials. Since Mother Teresa had only a passport from India and no visa, the officials could not allow her to enter the country. When we protested that this unassuming woman was a candidate for the Nobel Peace Prize, our strategy did not work the expected miracle.

Our luck didn't change when we told the officials that Mother Teresa was a world-famous nun — good, peaceful, saintly. In Spain, the law is the law. And the customs agent, understandably, was there to see that the law was followed.

Of course, the customs agent had a superior somewhere in the airport. And the airport manager also had to clear security matters with higher-ups.

Our problem was to reach the right person, which wasn't easy at that early hour of the morning.

To be as helpful as possible, one of the customs officials went off to present our case over the phone to a bureau chief. While we waited for an answer, we found Mother Teresa being interviewed by two reporters and a photographer. We explained the situation as best we could.

After a short wait the officer in charge came back with good news. "You're in luck," he told us. "Mother Teresa can stay in Spain for 24 hours without a visa."

Thus there was no need to tell him what we had discovered in the meantime: Mother Teresa was carrying a passport from the Vatican. She shows this passport only when the one from India proves insufficient. Mother Teresa will never give up her Indian citizenship. So the Vatican, through the influence of the late Pope Paul VI, had granted her a second, complimentary citizenship.

With that second passport, every door in Spain would have opened wide for Mother Teresa. But we were left with the feeling that she carried her Indian passport with much love and pride.

Agnes Gonxha Bojaxhiu was born on August 27, 1910. She was not born in India, but of Albanian parents in the city of Skopje, which is in Yugoslavia. When she made her religious vows in 1931, her fervent devotion to Saint Therese of the Child Jesus (Ste. Thérèse de Lisieux) led her to take the name of the Little Flower. (Mother Teresa sees Teresa of Avila as too great a model for herself.)

Until the age of 12 Agnes led an average life, like that of other girls in Skopje. Because there were no Catholic schools in the city, she went to a public school, but also attended classes at her parish. At meetings of the Sodality of Mary, the pastor would read letters by two missionaries from Yugoslavia who were serving in India. Agnes Gonxha followed the stories they told with ever-increasing interest, an interest which would gradually flower into a longing to serve as a missionary. But for the time being, she was happy at home with her parents and her older brother and sister whom she loved deeply.

When she was 12 years old, Agnes was blessed with the opportunity to meet one of the letter-writing missionaries on a rare visit to his homeland. Agnes listened with rapture as the

Jesuit priest told of his adventures in remote, picturesque India. Suddenly, her attention focused on one expression the priest used without much emphasis: "Each person, in life, has to follow his own road."

Never before had it occurred to the young girl that her own road might take her far from Skopje where she had always been so happy. Now, however, a disquieting yet joyful impulse struck her: the desire to become a missionary! As Agnes left the classroom where she had heard the missionary's words, her whole mind and spirit were filled with the refrain, *Follow your own road.* Was hers to be a road that would branch off from those her contemporaries would choose? Was she really meant to be a missionary?

Days later, Agnes put these questions to the Jesuit who had inspired her. The priest advised her to wait for the confirmation which time — and the voice of God — would give.

Teresa of Calcutta has never doubted that the voice of God reached to the very depths of her being. The desire to give herself in the service of her neighbors was so strong it never left her. The desire grew until, six years later when she was 18, the Jesuit missionary in whom she had confided returned to the town.

Agnes Gonxha confided in him once again, revealing her strong desire to become a missionary, possibly in India. This time the Jesuit told her of some Irish nuns who worked mainly in India. He said he would recommend her to their order. Agnes Gonxha knew she was now on the right path. She accepted the priest's offer with much joy.

The reply of the Irish nuns was positive: Agnes was welcomed to the postulate of the Sisters of Our Lady of Loreto at their motherhouse in Rathfarnham, near Dublin.

Agnes remained in Ireland for a year as a postulant. The purpose of this postulant year was to test and develop the young aspirants to religious life. In Agnes' case, this year-long period was an opportunity to learn a completely new language.

After the year of postulancy, Agnes was sent to India for her novitiate. When this second year ended, she made the religious vows — poverty, chastity, and obedience — on a temporary basis. She was to renew these vows every year, until she took her final vows in 1937.

During those eight years Agnes came to feel completely at home in India and completed a rigorous training. She received a post as teacher at Saint Mary's High School in Calcutta, run by her order, and soon rose to become its principal.

If Mother Teresa has a first love, it is teaching. Her students felt this love and repaid her with affection, respect, and, very often, a desire to emulate her.

3
The Call of the Poor

*"You don't have to look for distress;
it is screaming at you."*
Samuel Beckett

Many who have undergone a mystical experience of conversion speak of it as something indescribable. Mother Teresa does not dwell on the analysis of this experience. She limits herself to calling it the "Day of the Inspiration." In her case, it was actually a night — the night of September 10, 1946.

Sister Teresa was on a hot, crowded train going from Calcutta to the cool hill country of Darjeeling. This was where she had spent her novitiate. She was returning there to take part in some spiritual exercises.

On this night, it seems, God was an impatient suitor for her heart.

We often assume that God favors the solitude of a church when communicating with his people. But in the case of those who have developed a deep interior life, a church setting is not always needed for close communion with the Lord. On the night of September 10, 1946, Sister Teresa was able to pray in a train compartment crowded with passengers. And God answered. Her intimate companions on that trip were visions: visions of people living in subhuman misery on the outskirts of Calcutta. Touched to the depths of her heart, Teresa blended those visions with profound outpourings of prayer.

Gunnar Myrdal once commented that those who are well off have developed an ability to pass through crowds of people living in the greatest misery, hardly noticing them. To ignore the suffering and needs of the poor, the old, the sick is a chronic human failing.

Sister Teresa, however, had not been able to get used to the sight of human misery. In her case, the experience gave rise to a compelling urge to do something for those human beings. Miserable though they were, for her they bore the stamp of Christ.

From that night on the train, Teresa was aware of an intense desire to do something more than she had already tried to do. After returning from the spiritual exercises at Darjeeling, she could not resist going to the Archbishop of Calcutta to ask for advice, perhaps even permission to work among the poor and suffering.

Archbishop Périer reflected quietly, then told Sister Teresa that he could not grant her permission. Her request seemed a bit premature and out of place. He advised her to wait, to give herself time to be sure of her own intuition.

Sister Teresa accepted the Archbishop's advice. "His answer could not have been different," she says. "A bishop has no obligation to authorize the request of the first nun who comes to him with a more or less sublime project, just because she thinks it is God's will."

She returned to her teaching firmly intending to follow the Archbishop's instructions.

Still, behind the comfortable walls, surrounded by impeccable uniforms and clean student faces at Saint Mary's High School, Sister Teresa kept seeing ever more urgent visions. It seemed to her that thousands of hands were outstretched to her, endlessly asking for something more.

There were the faces of nameless derelicts dying in the streets; untouchables whose filthy, diseased bodies no one would go near; outcasts who, in their neglected condition, seemed to have lost all trace of human feeling.

These apparitions of the city slums were sights that would not leave her, even inside the convent where she was so happy. The tragic appeals of these desperate souls pursued her, pleading for help. With every day, she became more certain of the rightness of her compelling desire.

After becoming fully convinced that her inspiration was from a holy source, Teresa went to the Archbishop again, asking permission to leave her teaching order. This time, he advised her to appeal to her Superior General.

She obeyed, sending a humble and frank letter to the motherhouse in Ireland.

In a few days, Sister Teresa received a loving answer: "If this is the will of God, I cannot but authorize you wholeheartedly. Always remember that you can count on the affection and esteem of all here. If some day, for whatever reason, you decide to turn back, we will welcome you once again as sisters."

Her superior's consent was invaluable to Sister Teresa. But it was still necessary for the competent authority, the Archbishop of Calcutta, to write to Rome for final permission.

Archbishop Périer dated his letter February 2, 1948, nearly two years after Sister Teresa had come to him with her request. The answer from

Pope Pius XII arrived on April 12. Sister Teresa was authorized to leave the Sisters of Loreto, but would remain a religious with the vows of poverty, chastity, and obedience.

It was not easy for Sister Teresa to leave the congregation in which she had been so happy. But four months later, on August 9, 1948, she took off the Loreto habit she had worn for almost twenty years and left the sisters she loved. Their love in return gave her strength to make this fateful decision.

Sister Teresa's first step was to take a practical course in hygiene with Mother Dengel's Medical Missionary Sisters in Patna. She knew she would need a basic knowledge of nursing in order to work in the disease-ridden slums. The nursing course took four months. Teresa returned to Calcutta on Christmas Eve — a gift from God to his suffering poor.

On her first day in Calcutta, Teresa picked up five children who had been abandoned. She brought them to what was euphemistically called a school. She taught the children in the open, sheltered only by tree branches amid the noise and filth of a public park.

That first Christmas spent away from the Sisters of Loreto was a time of trial. Those first five children turned into twenty-five on Christmas Day. By New Year's Eve, there were forty-one of them under Mother Teresa's wing. None of them knew even the alphabet. But there were more urgent lessons to be learned: the basic rules of hygiene. These children were a world apart from the privileged middle class Mother Teresa had taught at Saint Mary's just a few months ago.

This was a difficult beginning for Sister Teresa. She was not far from where the Loreto Sisters lived, but there was now an enormous gulf between them. She experienced moments of terrible anguish and loneliness. Recalling those days, she said: "I had the feeling of how unbearable their poverty must be, for many. While looking for a house or shelter I would go searching without a destination, and my arms and legs would become exhausted. I thought how much the hearts and bodies of those who search for a house, food, or health must ache. The memory of the convent of Loreto became a temptation for my spirit. I freed myself from that anguish by a prayer that came from the bottom of my soul: *My God, I choose freely and because I love you, to remain faithful to my decision, and to do only your will.*"

During an interview (something she does not especially care for), Mother Teresa was asked to recall the beginnings of her work. She related one incident which speaks for itself:

"On my first trip along the street of Calcutta, after leaving Loreto, a priest came up to me. He asked me to give a contribution to a collection for the press. I had left the house with five rupees, and I had given four of them to the poor. I hesitated, then gave the priest the one I had left. That afternoon, the same priest came to see me and brought an envelope. He told me that a man had given him the envelope because he had heard about my projects and wanted to help me. There were 50 rupees in the envelope. I had the feeling, at that moment, that God had begun to bless the work and would never abandon me."

4
At Your Service, Mother

*"It takes only one good woman
to overcome a city."*
Saint Francis de Sales

Today, when many religious orders are going through a severe crisis, the congregation founded by Mother Teresa is flourishing. Paradoxically, the founding itself seems to have been almost accidental.

Mother Teresa never thought that what she had begun to do would attract attention. Nor did she ever think that anyone else would wish to live like her. Though it was *her* calling, she did not see her work as a model for others. Since the very beginning, however, this remarkable woman has had a powerful charisma that attracts people to herself.

Shortly after moving into an attic room donated by a state official, Michael Gomes, Mother Teresa was visited by Subhasini Das, a former student from Saint Mary's.

Mother Teresa told the young lady how her interest had shifted to the poorest of the poor. As she spoke, she seemed to radiate the perpetual springtime of a heart united to God.

Attracted by such grace, the young girl felt a strong desire to work with Mother Teresa. Could she place herself at Mother Teresa's disposal in service to the poor?

A few days later, on the feast of Saint Joseph, in 1949, Subhasini Das joined Mother Teresa in her work among the poor, choosing the name Agnes as a tribute.

Soon more girls followed, until there were ten of them — all former students of Sister Teresa.

The new congregation was approved on October 7, 1950. Mother Teresa did not take long to give it a name: Missionaries of Charity. Nor did she need much time to formulate the order's purpose: to be carriers of Christ's love in the slums.

Mother Teresa wasted little time in designing the habit the Sisters would wear. She simply adopted the Indian *sari,* the common dress of most women in Calcutta. "The *sari,*" she explains, "allows the Sisters to feel poor among the poor, to identify with the sick, with the children, with the homeless aging, and to share in the way of life of the dispossessed of this world by sharing in the same dress."

There are very fashionable and luxurious *saris.* For herself and her Sisters, Mother Teresa chose the most common type, made of the poorest fabric.

Eventually, that *sari* would become a well-known sight around the world. But for the moment, there was work to be done in Calcutta.

One day in 1952, Mother Teresa was making her usual rounds, searching the streets for people in need, when she came upon a shocking sight: a woman lying in a pile of rubbish, half eaten by rats and ants.

She seemed more a corpse than a person. The only sign of life Mother Teresa could detect in the woman was a weak cry: "To think my own son threw me here!"

Mother Teresa picked up the poor woman and took her to the nearest hospital. When they arrived, Mother Teresa was told that the hospital would not admit the woman. They accepted only curable patients, not the hopeless and dying. Mother Teresa answered that she would not move from the building if they did not admit the dying woman. Mother Teresa finally got her way. But the hospital staff did not succeed in keeping the woman alive.

Mother Teresa walked away from that hospital with an unquenchable desire to change the fate of such people. She went straight to the Calcutta health department, pleading for an end to such horrible neglect. She became such a strong advocate for the dying that city officials offered her the Darmashalah (Pilgrim's Hostel) which was next door to the temple of the goddess Kali, the protectress of the city.

The hostel consisted of two big rooms joined by a small hallway. The noises of cars mixed with the yelling of beggars and peddlers filtered through the windows along with dim rays of sunlight.

Mother Teresa renamed the building: *Nirmal Hriday* — Immaculate Heart.

It did not take her long to fill the house with dying people.

The Brahmin priests who conducted worship of the goddess Kali did not react kindly to the new situation. They considered Mother Teresa's activity a profaning of their sacred place. They began to spy on the nun. One of the priests had the task of keeping her in sight at all times. If the opportunity presented itself, he was to get rid of her, even if it entailed the use of violence.

Mother Teresa soon learned of these activities. Seeing danger for the people she was helping, she confronted the priest in charge and told him: "If you wish, you can kill me right here and now. But don't harm the poor dying."

The Hindu priest was jolted by this experience. It confirmed a report his spy had given him a short time before: Far from profaning the goddess Kali, this woman seems like the goddess herself. Do not harm her in any way.

"From that point on," says Mother Teresa, "we became friends. And the friendship deepened when one of the priests had tuberculosis. No hospital would accept him. But we did all we could to cure him.

"His companions came to see him. At first, the sick man blasphemed against God because of his desperate condition. But this behavior did not deter us from giving him our best care. His attitude changed, little by little, to the point of asking for a blessing before his death, which was very peaceful.

"His companions could not understand what had happened. From that point on, the priests of the goddess Kali never stopped showing us their friendship and offering us their help in many instances."

5
Christ in the Poor

"What the Lord wants is works."
Saint Teresa of Avila

In order to share life more completely with her beloved poor in Calcutta, Mother Teresa became a citizen of her adopted country, India.

After becoming an Indian citizen, Mother Teresa received closer cooperation from government agencies. But that is not why she did it. Her sole motive was to identify with the poor. India has known shocking poverty throughout its history. Before the time of Christ, so the story goes, the young Buddha left his palace grounds one day. He was so appalled by the human misery he saw outside the walls that he immediately gave up the life of a prince and became a homeless monk. Since that time, India's poverty has remained.

Let us look at the India of the present.

The annual income of a middle-class American is fifty times greater than that of a person in India.

An entire city in India could be fed with what is thrown away by a city in the Western world with the same population.

"A hungry man, an angry man," is a proverb. But in India, while the average person is hungry, he is not angry.

Hatred between the rich and poor is virtually nonexistent in India. A richly dressed man or woman can walk through the slums of Calcutta or New Delhi without arousing the least hostility from the teeming masses of poor people.

The people of India are peaceful; they live resigned to their poverty. They believe their lot in life is a "deserved condition." This belief is so ingrained that the people of India do not even try to free themselves from poverty.

This fatalism is the result of thousands of years of religious tradition.

So the tragic social conditions in India are not due to disorganization or passivity, as it might seem to the Western eye. It results from their Hindu interpretation of life. The people believe that there is one single spirit which permeates all beings, including plants and animals, and that all existence is united by this life-giving spirit.

This conviction leads the people not to harm animals in any way — especially cows, which Indians consider sacred animals. Mahatma Gandhi once confessed that his mother had refused to kill a poisonous serpent discovered in their patio at home. She would not harm the spirit within it.

The *ātman,* or true self, within each human being has a never-ending life. Death, in this view, is merely the passing of the human soul to a nonphysical plane and, after a time, back into another human body.

Human souls do not die. They migrate from body to body until they reach the point of final liberation (*mokṣa*).

Existence, according to Hindu philosophy, is an uninterrupted wheel (*samsāra*) of birth and rebirth, or reincarnation. Each person is reborn into a condition earned by the uprightness or sinfulness of his previous existence. According to tradition believed by many Hindus, a person's caste, or social class, depends on the *karma* the person has accumulated during previous lives. Whoever has lived justly is reincarnated into a higher caste.

Though very complex, with a variety of regional differences throughout India, the caste system can be viewed as having four classes of people: brahmins (the highest, priestly class), warriors, businessmen, and laborers. Outside and beneath these castes is the group known as *pariahs,* the untouchables. Though legally equal to other citizens in modern India, pariahs are at the bottom of the social ladder.

According to popular belief, the *brahmins* enjoy their privileged status for having lived good lives in previous existences. They have a good *karma*.

The *pariahs* suffer the punishment of having lived sinfully in previous existences. But they are resigned. They do not rebel against this situation because they think they deserve it. To rebel would mean taking a risk, perhaps being reincarnated in an even more degrading condition.

One major result of this socio-religious system is that the economic situation is improving very slowly. Sad though this is, we must understand that the root cause of India's massive poverty is the people's constant quest for the highest spiritual values. The outsider's scornful judgment, based on the materialistic mentality of the Western world, could be considered presumptuous as well as unjust.

Among the host of material evils that pariahs contend with, there is one that always haunts them. That is the terrible evil of hunger.

Their suffering is acute. Hunger is an evil that hovers over the entire country, particularly in Calcutta. Here, for example, the income per capita is five times less than in New Delhi; ten times less than in Bombay.

When the poor in Calcutta can no longer stand the pain of hunger, they make a last futile effort to eat. They line the streets as beggars.

Tourists report: "The charity of a handout is more useless here than almost anywhere else on earth." They advise that no alms be given in order to avoid a whole cluster of beggars around the donor, blocking his way.

When they are rejected, the beggars look for scraps of rubbish and garbage. As in other poverty-ridden nations, many women try to escape hunger by becoming prostitutes.

Sometimes the poor masses can queue up for rice. But during the frequent periods of famine, the daily ration is only 160 grams (roughly a half cup) per person. The lines stretch interminably. When the word goes out that there is no more rice, there is sudden panic in the line. Then, slowly, reluctantly, the line breaks up. The next day there will be a new line, and the same fear.

Those who can, by some desperate means, will buy rice in the black market at a price three times higher than the official one.

Even in India there is a rich harvest from profiteering in human misery. Even in these squalid surroundings there are distinguished gentlemen who maintain their wealth at the expense of others.

The poor, meanwhile, keep living the mystery of human life. "Blessed are the poor," said Jesus. Mother Teresa says:

"The poor are great people. They give us much more than we give them. We have learned many things from them. They don't need our pity. They need our love and compassion.

"Some time ago a man came to our house and told me that a Hindu family with eight children had not eaten for many days. So I took some rice and I went to the family and I saw the little faces with the large dark eyes. Real hunger! And the mother took the rice from my hand and she divided it into two and she went out. When she came back I asked her, 'What did you do?' She said, 'They are hungry also.' The next-door neighbor, a Muslim family, was hungry and she knew that she had the courage and the love to share."

Perhaps, one day, someone will write for the world the dramatic story of the first months of Mother Teresa's Missionaries of Charity. Those first days seem almost unbelievable. Mother Teresa lived in an attic. She had no funds, no food, no prospect of surviving alone. When she did receive a mite of food, or a few rupees, she used the contribution to satisfy the needs of the poor before she took care of herself.

The amazing thing is that the Sisters who follow her today do not have it much better than she did at that time. Their sacrifice is equal to hers.

"Our rigorous poverty is our safeguard," says Mother Teresa. "We do not want to do what other religious orders have done throughout history, and begin by serving the poor only to end up unconsciously serving the rich. In order to understand and help those who have nothing, we must live like them . . . the only difference is that these people are poor by birth, and we are poor by choice. It is nonetheless true that without the conviction that it is Christ Himself that we see in the outcasts, such a lifestyle would be impossible.''

The Sisters are not spoiled. Their daily routine is a difficult one that varies little from one continent to the other.

They rise very early in the morning. They do their personal chores. They pray and attend Mass, then have breakfast. As soon as possible, they leave for their work. They hurry to the home of the dying, to dispensaries, schools, hospitals for lepers, or go on field trips to pick up the dying and abandoned children from the streets. They visit families where there are sick people, or lonely rooms where an old person, unattended, is desperate for a human word.

In the 1970s, Jesuit Father J. H. McCown traveled and worked in East Africa. His book, *Elephants Have the Right of Way*, describes the life of the Sisters in Tabora, Tanzania. He writes:

"The Sisters sleep on pallets all in the same small room. They own nothing you couldn't put into a cigar box. They eat exactly the same food they beg and prepare for their poor people. There are five of them. They are lovely. Young, delicate, exquisite, they captivate with their soft brown eyes and gentle manner. I am greeted warmly. Later I meet them in a tiny chapel where a black ebony Christ looks tenderly from a cross behind the altar; above Him are the words, I THIRST.

"I am shown around the compound. Old women, weak and emaciated, several blind, sit in the shade against the cool mud walls and call to us as we pass. A little boy with huge head and spiderlike body crawls across the yard slowly and with cataleptic preoccupation examines a handful of sand he picks up. He is an unwanted child whom the nuns found nearly dead from malnutrition. A young albino woman greets us cheerfully when she hears us coming. Her poor body, with skin devoid of protective pigment, is covered with sun sores; and her eyes, recently scalded from exposure, are covered with heavy yellow bandages.

"Sister Damien introduces me to their little leper who comes every day for food and medication; she is a pleasant young woman with stumps for fingers but otherwise unravaged by the disease.

"They take me to their camp, another place for paupers that a willing civil administration allows them to service. Here 100 old men and women greet us enthusiastically. The nuns speak Swahili well enough to talk to each pitiful old person sweetly, to discuss their aches and pains, to change bandages, to measure out doses of medicine. On other days they come to bathe the more helpless old people. The nuns are radiant and there is much merriment as they go from patient to patient. There is no leprosy here in the camp but there are several cases of yaws which seems worse to me and advanced cases of elephantiasis. Everybody shakes hands with everybody else. The nuns are as demonstrative and affectionate as if they had been dealing with sweet-smelling children. I washed my hands for an hour when I got back home. Of stout stuff I am not made!. . .

"The Sisters accept with literalness the words of Christ. They enjoy the 'little things of this world' at about the same level as their people. I ask them what I can get for them . . . only some medicines for their poor."

It is difficult for the observer to understand how they are able to stay so serenely happy in the midst of so much suffering. Only Mother Teresa herself can explain their feelings: "It is with joy that we must contact Christ under His mask of wretchedness, because joy is love. Joy is a prayer; joy is strength; joy is a net of love in which you can catch souls." All who work with Mother Teresa, or assist her in any way, seem to learn this simple art of spreading love and joy.

While I was gathering information for this book, I came across one Missionary of Charity who still had her teaching license. She was not from India (even though the majority of Mother Teresa's Sisters are from India); she was from the West.

She was also — if I may mention my honest appreciation — very good-looking. She did not seem shy. On the contrary, she was natural and spontaneous, completely in command of herself.

She started to explain the work she and the other Sisters were doing, and to talk about Mother Teresa. I interrupted, asking her to be more personal. Why did she give up the world for a religious life? Especially such a demanding one? She answered without hesitation: "Three years ago my decision to enter the Missionaries of Charity matured. Of course, I have encountered difficulties, but I knew them before I asked to be admitted. I feel happy here. I believe that today's youth, not very abundant in generosity or enthusiasm, would have many reasons for loving Mother Teresa's work, if only they knew more about it.''

She told me that the training of a Missionary of Charity is not very long, but it is intense.

There are six months of aspirancy to test each new arrival. The psychological and emotional stability of the candidates is usually one of the qualities that is considered basic. That is why Mother Teresa accepts more readily young women who have reached a certain degree of maturity rather than adolescents who are still insecure and inconstant.

Basic generosity is also a highly valued trait. So is the ability to learn languages. (English is the official language of the congregation, since it is the *lingua franca* of India.) However, it is not essential that a girl know English when she enters as long as she has the desire and ability to learn it.

In addition to religious formation, the aspirant also receives a cultural formation. After the six months of aspirancy, there follow six more months of postulancy. The newcomer is introduced to the rich spiritual life of a Missionary of Charity.

Then comes the novitiate — two years of spiritual preparation for religious community life. At the end of these two years, candidates take the three vows of obedience, chastity, and poverty, plus a fourth vow of wholehearted and free service to the poorest of the poor.

Mother Teresa says: ''The Missionary of

Charity has to give. But, above all, she has to give of herself."

The new Sister will find few decorations in the chapels of the institution. There is always a crucifix, a plain one. By the side of each cross, one inscription is seen: "I thirst."

The life of Mother Teresa's Sisters is a life rooted in the Gospel. They strive to fulfill faithfully the words of Christ: "I was hungry and you gave me food. I was thirsty and you gave me drink. I was naked and you clothed me. I was ill and you comforted me. As often as you did it for one of my least brothers, you did it for me."

For the Missionaries of Charity, Christ is personified in the poor. In the poor and with the poor, He is hungry and thirsty. With them and in them He is sick and naked. With them and in them He needs shelter.

In the words of Mother Teresa: "He is the poor Jesus, the hungry Jesus, the thirsty Jesus, the naked Jesus."

They make Tertullian's words their own: "You have seen your brother, you have seen your God."

They truly feel that each person they deal with is Christ. And this is not the product of self-suggestion in order to make matters easier. It is the genuine fruit of a faith which does not falter in responding to Christ's affirmation, "What you do for the least of my brothers, you do for me."

Of course, the Gospel has inspired many people in every age and has given meaning to the sacrifices made in Christ's name. But many feel that no group, since the days of Saint Francis and his little Brothers, has given itself so totally to the

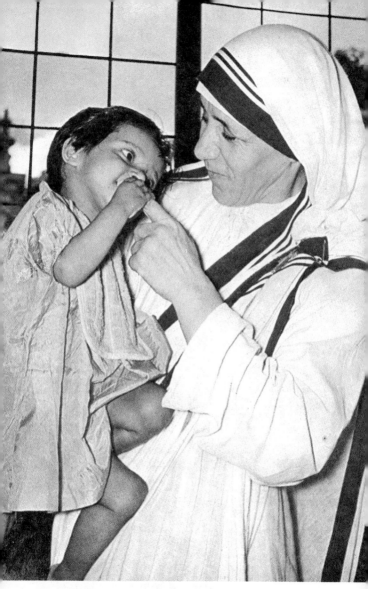

Mother Teresa and friend. For this picture, as for the rest
of Mother Teresa's life, there was no posing.

Jacqueline de Decker, Mother Teresa's paralyzed friend
and spiritual godmother. *Right:* Brother Andrew, first
Servant (superior) of the Missionary Brothers of Charity.
Below: Pope Paul VI approves the "Co-Workers of Mother
Teresa."

Mother Teresa and Brazil's Dom Helder Camara: two lives committed to serving Christ in the poorest of the poor.

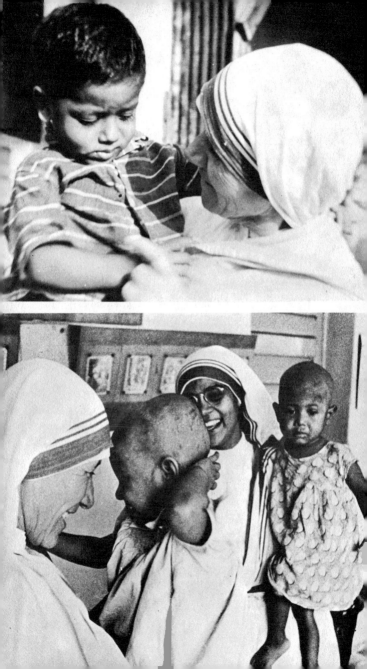

The Missionaries of Charity draw strength from prayer for their service of Christ in the poor. *Below:* Mother Teresa comforts a dying man.

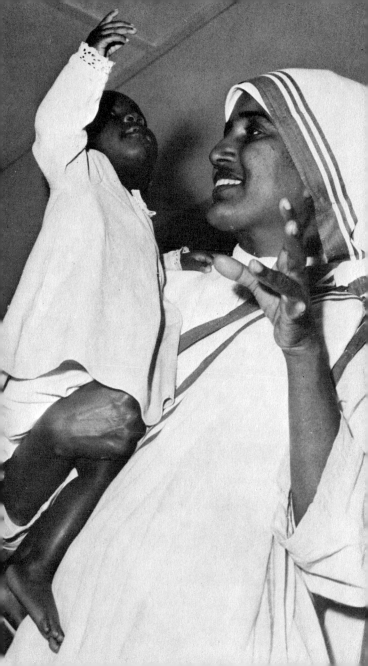

CORPORATION OF CALCUTTA
NIRMAL HRIDAY
HOME FOR DYING DESTITUTES

কলিকাতা পৌর প্রতিষ্ঠান
নির্মল হৃদয়
মুমূর্ষু নিরাশ্রয়দের আশ্রয়স্থান

Christian ideal as have the Missionaries of Charity.

The proof is in the extraordinary impact they have had in the world. Good is contagious. "A great change is coming about now," says Mother Teresa. "The rich are coming to wash and feed the poor!" Mother Teresa and her Sisters have avoided the great error of trying to convince others that they are wrong in their beliefs, and that the truth belongs exclusively to her order. In the tradition and culture of India, any such approach is sure to result in disaster.

In India there exists the most sacred respect and tolerance for the convictions of others. Just the same, non-Indians often attempt to convince the natives that their own convictions are wrong. This explains the antagonism many authorities in India have against most missionary efforts of other religions.

Mother Teresa and her Sisters know this psychology well. It suits their emphasis on works rather than on theological discourse. Yet, there is no doubt that the religious convictions of the Missionaries of Charity run deep. How else would they have the strength to carry out such superhuman tasks?

Mother Teresa and her Sisters see the agonizing Christ in the abandoned and ignored.

They see Christ fleeing to Egypt in the refugees that flee from persecution and violence.

They identify the Babe in the manger in Bethlehem with the faces of thousands of abandoned children.

No matter whom they go near, they always bring an overflowing and sincere love to the individual. They come as close as they would get to Christ Himself.

They live their faith and their charity as something natural and spontaneous. The fact that most of the people they deal with are not Christian does not distract them from their errand of mercy, sponging the wounds of Christ. They are more interested in seeing Hindus become better Hindus and Muslims better followers of Allah.

Truly, lack of tolerance and a spirit of fanaticism are more often the signs of weakness than of a strong faith. Spiritual leaders such as John XXIII, Pedro Arrupe, Roger Schutz, and José Maria de Llanos — like Mother Teresa herself — know how to be tolerant in the truest sense.

For that very reason they give the most eloquent and winning testimony to their own beliefs. Tolerance and respect for the beliefs of others are characteristic of true religious fervor. In a land where a deep interest in religious teaching is centuries-old, the people of India respect Mother Teresa and her Sisters for their tolerance and understanding.

Even government officials, who resist and even expel other missionaries, join in this respect and admiration for Mother Teresa's work. Although she is a foreigner by birth, they see her as a person who is deeply identified with the Indian soul, a person in touch with the traditions and culture of her adopted land.

6
Brothers and Contemplatives

"We must love one another or die."
W. H. Auden

The magnetism that drew young women to Mother Teresa's work soon attracted young men. As the men came to her, one by one, she entrusted them with care of the dying and of boys in her schools.

When a nucleus of nine men had formed, Mother Teresa founded the Missionary Brothers of Charity. For the first three years, she herself led the new group as they did various kinds of work with the poor of Calcutta. Eventually an Australian priest, now called Brother Andrew, became General Servant (or superior) of the Missionary Brothers. (Like all the members of the congregation, he is called Brother. Known formerly as Father Ian Travers-Ball, he changed his name to Andrew when he joined the Missionaries of Charity.) Asked why he accepted Mother Teresa's invitation to spend his life in this way, Brother Andrew answered simply: "The need is so evident."

The Missionary Brothers are less numerous than Mother Teresa's Missionary Sisters. But their life is the same: self-sacrifice for the suffering poor — in a spirit of serene happiness. The Brothers have been able to enter areas of work that are less suited to the Sisters. In some cities, for example, the Brothers live in the slums and work with destitute alcoholics.

Typical of the Brothers' work and spirit is the following letter from Brother Jeremy:

"Here in Los Angeles, we have four communities and twenty-five Brothers. Our first house was Edgeware Road. It flourishes today with a community of four Brothers who work among the poor Latino families in the area. They visit those most in need, run a community center at which women can sew, get clothes for their families, and also receive the vegetables, bread, and many other foods thrown out by the markets of the city. They are also able to take in a small number of homeless or runaway boys until other arrangements are made.

"Our Brothers at our Cambria Street Community offer hospitality to about twenty men who are homeless. The men can get clean clothes, a shower or a place for the night, but, more importantly, it is a place to BE — to be accepted, to be wanted, to be loved. Although the faces change, it is, in short, a HOME. About another fifty men come once a day for a noontime meal. With all this activity in the house the Brothers here have somehow managed to continue to reach out to the poor families in the neighborhood who are in need.

"In Santa Ana we have another house of hospitality. Our four Brothers there have room for about twenty-five people in need of emergency shelter. Most are women and children, with some entire families arriving who would be sleeping in a park or a car if this were not available. Here we have just begun to reach out slowly to the families around us.

"Here at St. Vincent's Community on Skid

Row we have our Novitiate House. Novices from five countries are here to be formed in the work and spirit of our Congregation. As part of their formation they work half of the day in the Skid Row area, visiting the old and the sick, the alcoholics and families in the rooms of the old hotels here, trying to be a loving and caring presence in a place where violence and alienation are much more ordinary.

"Our work is small in comparison to the vast numbers who are in need. The similarities of our Community here and in Calcutta are striking. In both cities there are large numbers of people dying unwanted and uncared for, whether on the streets of Calcutta or downtown Los Angeles. There are the lepers — be they actual lepers or the 'social lepers' who are our alcoholics and street people; the children and the terrible conditions under which they live in both places. We feel over-whelmed at times at how small our efforts are in relationship to the need. However, we can only try to keep in mind that we are simply the instruments God is using, and if we only let him, he can do marvelous things through these small Communities of love. In his total plan then we need not worry about the numbers we can't reach, we need only be here, love here, and believe that the good news of God's love will reach those most crushed, lonely, and frightened.

"And here where we encounter life in its most bruised and broken forms, we sometimes get a glimpse of the miracle of love in these very same lives. We are blessed to see the seemingly broken who are healed, the seeming sinner who is a saint, the seeming poor man who is rich in ways we could never imagine. Yes, God has blessed us. He brought us here today to witness the miracle of his presence born anew in the hearts of the poor. He is here among us, disguised in rags and dirt. It is he — hungry; it is he — thirsty; it is he — homeless and lonely. It is he, in Los Angeles, who walks the streets so disguised as even to be shocking to us.

"We are grateful to be here to feed Jesus, hungry and thirsty; to clothe and shelter Jesus, cold and homeless; to embrace and love Jesus, broken and lonely."

Speaking of the Missionaries' work, Brother Andrew says:

"There are many and very deep comforts that come from working among the suffering poor. There is a great satisfaction that comes from seeing human beings alleviated, at least for a while, from their pain . . . sick people who recover their health, families who find work to earn a living, abandoned children who find shelter and respond to love like human beings, alcoholics and drug addicts who are able to overcome the most difficult temptations."

Outside India, the Missionary Brothers of Charity have houses in the United States, Hong Kong, Taiwan, Korea, Guatemala, El Salvador, Japan, and Macao.

No matter where they are, the Brothers experience Christ in a way that comes only from love of the poor. This incident related by Brother Andrew is a good example:

"A few days ago we came across a man and his five-year-old son cowering on the railway plat-form at the station. They were malnourished, shivering, deathly sick. The man's wife was already dead, lying by his side. We picked them up, without knowing which ones were alive or dead, and we took them home. The father died a few days later, without ever speaking. But the child stopped coughing little by little and started getting better. Now, he has begun to smile and to play with the other children who have been picked up under similar circumstances and helped with the same gifts of food, medicine, and love. I cannot tell you of the feelings I experience at this moment, while I picture such children, this child and another with a leg missing, also picked up at the same railway station . . . now playing happily at my side.''

Serving the abandoned poor helps the Brothers to see Jesus through the eyes of Jesus. Brother Andrew's touching words about the death of Johnny Walker gave us a glimpse of that vision:

''Among the many events this year, there died in Calcutta one of the most successful men I have ever known. I mentioned him before in my letters when he was a little boy of five years playing around the table as I was trying to write. He had a stiff leg and something was missing from his mind. The Sisters had found him on the streets, and he said, 'My name is Johnny Walker' — a name he or we never changed. He was thrown out as a child, crippled, low I.Q., couldn't learn to read. And yet he was so joyful and happy always, ever ready with a funny song or dance to bring joy to others. He had no anger. I spoke about him in Malcolm Muggeridge's film and book, *Something Beautiful for God,* as making other boys with sad stories laugh and forget, and thousands all over the world heard of him. He would pray each day with the other boys and come to Mass on Sundays. He would join his hands and bow his head. He knew that God was present. And he knew that love and joy and a smile are at the heart of God. So Johnny died at 18, drowned in a few inches of water when he had an unexpected seizure. Now he is a saint — after a joyful, successful life if ever there was one. Just the thought of Johnny's life and death strengthens me and rejoices me as it does the many to whom I tell his story.''

Shortly before Archbishop Oscar Romero was murdered while celebrating Mass in San Salvador on March 24, 1980, Brother Jeremy wrote the following note. Without saying so, Jeremy's words show that the Missionary Brothers are willing to lay down their lives for the poor. Jeremy wrote:

"In June of 1979 our first Brothers went to El Salvador to begin in some small way to serve the people of this poor and oppressed land. We have three Brothers there who live in one of the most densely populated parts of the capital, San Salvador. In the last year both priests in their parish have been shot to death. Along with the terrible poverty comes the violence and uncertainty of this time in El Salvador's history. The three Missionary of Charity Brothers are only just beginning to meet the people, be trusted by them and to serve them. Their small presence seems so little in view of the great problems facing the people. But it is with a deep belief in the parables of Jesus about the *seed* and its eventual fruit that impels us to go there. At times such as these, I suspect that our presence as communities of love and peace amid the violence and destruction of war means far more than we at first perceive. In a special way I ask for your prayers for this small community of Brothers. May it be a sign of hope and an oasis of love and peace for the abandoned and broken people we meet there."

The Sisters and Brothers experience a happiness that flows from their love of human beings whom society rejects. The source of that love they find in prayer. Mother Teresa deeply believes that prayer gives her Missionaries the love and strength to lessen the suffering of humanity.

The Missionaries of Charity spend at least two hours a day at community prayer. But that is not all. Mother Teresa constantly seeks new resources for deepening divine charity.

The most dynamic resource she has tapped is contemplative prayer. In 1976, on the feast of the Sacred Heart, Mother Teresa established a second group of Sisters in New York — the Missionaries of Charity Contemplative. The mission of these Sisters is to live "God's word through eucharistic adoration and contemplation and to proclaim the Word of God to the poorest of the poor by their presence and spiritual works of mercy" so that the Word made flesh "will remain in the hearts of men."

Soon after the Contemplative Sisters were founded, Mother Teresa took the next step. She established a contemplative branch of men in Rome.

The Sisters and Brothers are not about to experience a power failure. Besides their own deep lives of prayer, their fellow Missionaries Contemplative supply them and the suffering poor with a boundless measure of charity.

7
Sowers of Joy

"Love builds, only love builds.
Hatred destroys."
Pope John Paul II

The Missionaries of Charity do not keep a detailed account for God of their service to the poorest of the poor. Nor do they take any credit for the heroic love and care they offer daily. They are concerned only with their daily work: tending the wounds of Christ.

Mother Teresa says, "Only in heaven will we fully realize how much we owe to the poor for helping us love God better through them."

Following the example of Mother Teresa, the Sisters have a single concern: helping human beings who are scorned and forsaken by society, those who can no longer even hope or dream.

But what, really, is Mother Teresa accomplishing? Is it true, as some suggest, that her work is just a drop in the bucket? Does it fail to deal with the real social evils of India?

Mother Teresa's answer is that planning and technology are not the universal medicine for all evils. Even if they were, she does not have the patience to wait for the perfect solution to the problems of the poor. In the logic of her charity, Mother Teresa considers that the *individual* is the only true value. Faced with the mass of starving and dying people, she does not see a crowd but simply a starving person. Only one. "I never think in terms of a crowd, only of one person. If I visualized a crowd I would never get started. What matters is the individual person.''

Planning and technology can be applied in many areas, but not in the area of love.

Mother Teresa and her Sisters know well that they will never satisfy all hunger, cure all wounds, provide all the shelter needed by the abandoned, the lepers, the hungry who struggle to exist in a terribly unjust world. But if they allowed this knowledge to deter them, thousands of dying people would never find a bed on which to die. Millions of sick people and lepers would never receive cures for their wounds and illnesses.

Mother Teresa's criterion differs from that of most people. The awareness that they cannot do everything does not keep them from trying to do as much as they can. And only God knows how much generous hearts such as Mother Teresa's and her Sisters' are capable of doing!

Addressing a group of Co-Workers one day, Mother Teresa said something that reflects her point of view. She said: ''The Sisters do small things. They help children. They visit the abandoned and the sick, people who live alone. A woman was found dead several days after her death in one of the houses they visit. Her body was already decomposed. The neighbors did not even know her name . . . . When someone argues that the Sisters have done no enormous task, that they merely do small things and people hardly notice their presence, I answer that even if they had helped only one human being, it would have been enough. Jesus would have died for just one person, for one sinner . . . .''

There is another way in which Mother Teresa's Sisters are unique.

Missionaries to the Third World have traditionally been priest and nuns from the richer nations. Mother Teresa's Sisters are daughters of that Third World. Most were born in India. And now they are going in ever-increasing numbers to the supposedly rich nations of the world. They are leaving the needs of their own people in India to help the poor in 66 other countries. They are now found in such supposedly rich cities as London, New York, Detroit, St. Louis, Caracas, Lima, Mexico City, Buenos Aires, Manila, Rotterdam, Essen, Madrid, and Rome. Obviously, the poverty that Mother Teresa tries to remedy in these great cities is not merely the lack of material goods. There are other kinds of deprivation. Mother Teresa says: "The worst disease today is not leprosy or tuberculosis, but rather the feeling of being unwanted, uncared for and deserted by everybody. The greatest evil is the lack of love and charity, the terrible indifference toward one's neighbor who lives at the roadside."

Such indifference is everywhere in this secular world.

The chairman of the International Association of Co-Workers of Mother Teresa tells about Mother Teresa's experiences in London. "When Mother Teresa came to London for an orientation which might lead to the opening of the first European novitiate of her congregation, we took her to see the night life around the capital. The tour was organized by the Simon Community, an aid group which takes care of people abandoned by society. We started the tour around Soho.

"In Saint Martin-in-the-Fields, we came across old people who were sleeping against the building grates, listening to the hum of the steam that was coming from the kitchens of restaurants and cafeterias.

"Later on, we went to sit in a nearby cafe, not far from Covent Garden. A meeting for drug addicts had just ended, but there was one young man who had not left. He looked at us with apparent scorn and, in front of Mother Teresa, put his hand in his pocket and took out a good number of barbiturates and swallowed them. Immediately, he fell to the ground.

"Mother Teresa was much concerned. Quickly, the members of the Simon Community picked the young man up and took him to an aid center. They searched his pockets and found a few prescriptions for heroin, some vials, syringes, and an empty bottle. They took his temperature and had doubts that he would survive.

"We continued our tour. There were many people sleeping along the wharves on the Thames who were covered with old newspapers. This was in December, almost Christmas. Mother Teresa was thoughtful: *Why did that young man, well-dressed and not materially poor, take so many pills? Why did so many people have to sleep outside? Was there a lack of love? Was it a reaction to the abandonment of others?*

"Mother Teresa turned to us, her eyes bright and almost luminous. She said, 'Money is not enough. It can only buy material things like food, clothing, and shelter. Something else is needed. There are evils that can't be remedied with money . . . only with love . . . .'"

There is a peace, a joy, and an authority about Mother Teresa that makes you hang on her words. And that is true also, to some extent, of her Sisters.

The Missionaries of Charity earn respect. They do not look for thanks or for material rewards for their difficult tasks. Instead, they know an intimate peace which they experience in their daily work. And sometimes they receive what they consider payments, one hundred times over, from the lips of the people they help.

One Sister received such an award from a man who was about to die. His last words were: "I have lived like an animal. I die like a human being."

Sometimes their reward is the burning gratitude in eyes about to close forever. Such an incident occurred when a poor beggar was picked up as he was dying in a pile of rubbish. He was reduced, by suffering and hunger, to a mere spectre of a man. Mother Teresa took him to the Home for the Dying and put him in bed. When she tried to wash him, she discovered that his body was covered with worms. Pieces of his skin were coming off as she washed him. For one brief moment, the man seemed to revive. In his semi-conscious state, he asked Mother Teresa, "Why do you do it?"

"For love . . . ."

The dying man could hardly smile his thanks. The half-smile remained on his lips as he closed his eyes forever.

The life of the Missionaries of Charity is one of heroic sacrifice. And yet, Mother Teresa's followers are happy, even joyous. This may help to explain their increase in vocations, at a time when vocations in other religious communities are in a state of decline.

Perhaps another reason for this abundance of vocations is that India has always given many of its sons and daughters to religious organizations. That is still true today. Out of 1,500 Missionaries of Charity, 90 percent are native Indians, from tribal groups as well as from the middle and upper classes.

"Don't you find your life too hard?" I asked one of them who was living in a European convent of the Missionaries of Charity. Before answering my rather indiscreet question, the Sister looked at me and smiled. "I knew," she told me, "before entering, that life here was like that. I do not desire any other."

"Yes, but . . . ."

Sister interrupted me. She must have known I had gotten a wrong impression. "It is the life that makes me happiest. I would not trade it for any other."

The Sisters are happy even from the beginning of their arduous training. Many are like one young lady who, during her novitiate training, had to spend half a day at the Home for the Dying. When she returned to the convent, she met Mother Teresa. Mother Teresa saw that she was beaming with happiness, and asked why she was so overjoyed. "Mother," the novice answered, "I have touched the body of Christ for the last three hours."

The work of the Missionaries of Charity is very hard from a human standpoint. One day some people told Mother Teresa that they would not do what she and her Sisters do even for a million dollars. Mother Teresa answered, "I would not do it for a million dollars either. Or for any amount. But I do it gladly for the love of Christ, to whom we direct our help under his disguise of the poor."

Mother Teresa does not see lack of material goods as the key factor in poverty. She stresses another more dramatic and intimate lack: the illness which results from the rejection by others. What the poor need — even before food, clothing, or shelter — is to be loved. The alienation which condemns them to their poverty is the deadliest part of their condition.

People who work with Mother Teresa's Sisters say that the Sisters seem to have a superhuman capacity to give themselves totally to others. Their Rule says: "We are to offer not only help but also our happy and peaceful smile to all who suffer, child or adult, abandoned or sick, dying or leper. The Missionary of Charity should not only offer material helps. She must do it with all her soul."

Joy seems to be the predominant expression on the face and in the gesture of every Sister. How can it be explained? It is the very heart and mystery of the Christian faith.

Certainly their joy is reinforced by a simple prayer they repeat often. It is addressed to Mary, "Cause of our joy, pray for us . . . ."

Mother Teresa proposes to her Sisters ideals that are equally challenging: "We should be angels of mercy and comfort. We should take the image of Christ as a friend of the little ones to the children of the slums. We should love the poor with the love of Christ. Help them with his same help. Give as he gives. Serve as he serves. Save as he saves.''

The Sisters make efforts to offer love, but not pity. Pity is somewhat arrogant because it comes, in a way, from looking down at others.

The attitude of the Missionaries of Charity comes from a deeper feeling. They consider the poorest of the poor as persons who are somehow more deserving than others. They are truly Christ under the guise of pain and poverty.

This is why the Sisters put their whole heart into everything they do. Even though they do not mean to, they often evoke the deepest feelings of gratitude and admiration from those they serve — feelings which had been buried by a lifetime of neglect and scorn from others.

It is not easy for a person to know and love God when that person has experienced the cruelest misery and scorn from his brothers and sisters. Fortunately, the witness of love by the Missionaries of Charity often helps people believe in a God who comforts and heals.

Mother Teresa does not like to talk about herself. Nor does she like others to focus attention on her. She does not think she deserves any special attention. As far as her work, she judges it with this logic: If it were her work and not God's, it would not have survived.

Basically, Mother Teresa does not even consider herself the foundress of the Missionaries of Charity. She considers herself only the human instrument of God's goodness for the poor. She often tells her Sisters, ''Our work would be no more than a mere social aid, as useful and needed as that is, if it were not saturated by our suffering. Our work has to be Christ's work. And Christ redeemed us only after accepting our human condition, our loneliness, our agony, our death.''

This does not mean that Mother Teresa teaches her Sisters to do good with a frown. She tells them, ''Isn't our work to give God to the poor in the worst slums? Can you give God without joy? The God we should communicate to others is a living God, a God of love. Words should emanate from our hearts, which give to men the joy of God.''

She adds, ''We should never allow anyone to go away from us without feeling better and happier. We should be like the reflection of God's goodness to the poor. We should always have a smile on our lips, a smile for each child we help, for each person who has been abandoned or is sick and to whom we give comfort and medicine. It would matter little if we only offered material gifts, we must offer our heart to all.''

Mother Teresa has another rule for her Sisters: ''We all have to see Christ in the poor. The more distasteful the work and the people seem, the greater and stronger should be our faith, our love and our self-giving in the service of our Lord in the poverty we see.''

She concludes: ''It is not what we do, but the love we put into what we do.''

8
The Great Limousine Raffle

"Where will Christ's love ever end?"
Pope Paul VI

One day, in the spring of 1968, Pope Paul VI sent a personal letter to Mother Teresa. Along with the letter were two round-trip airplane tickets from Calcutta to Rome, and a check for $10,000.

This was not the first nor the last time that the Pope sent money to Mother Teresa. But why plane tickets to Rome?

The reason was simple: Pope Paul VI was inviting Mother Teresa to start a new community of Sisters in Rome itself. Even Rome, the Eternal City, has slums that cry out for the healing presence of Mother Teresa's Missionaries.

Mother Teresa and Sister Frederick used the two airline tickets on August 22, 1968. They landed in Rome unnoticed among hundreds of passengers. The only person on hand to greet them was a papal emissary.

Unlike most newcomers, Mother Teresa and Sister Frederick did not ask to see Rome's historic monuments. Instead, they asked for directions to the nearest slum. After a brief tour, they realized that misery was indeed a reality in Rome. In Mother Teresa's words, "There was an act of love to be done there."

She and her Sisters accepted the Pope's invitation to open a new house in Rome.

The Missionaries of Charity receive such invitations regularly from bishops throughout the world. In each case they make a careful study of the actual need. They never go to a new place unless invited. But once they see that they are needed, they act quickly to answer the call.

The typical house the Missionaries live in is a hovel that is no different from the lodgings of the very poor. Even before looking for shelter for themselves, the Sisters always look first for shelter for others — the dying, the sick, the orphans, the abandoned.

In 1965 when the Sisters arrived in Venezuela to open their first house outside of India, they were preceded by the generosity of some local citizens. These kind people had prepared a luxurious home for the Sisters. It had a refrigerator, an electric washer, and comfortable furniture. Mother Teresa had accompanied the Sisters who were there to start the new house. When Mother Teresa saw how luxurious the place was, her reaction was typical. She changed it into a simple dwelling for the Sisters.

When a group of us had to look for a house for the first Sisters in Spain, we looked long and hard. There were hundreds of places for sale or rent in residential neighborhoods. But in the deprived areas where the Sisters were going to work, nothing was available. That left us with a problem, because the Sisters had no intention of moving into a nice neighborhood. We had heard how austere Mother Teresa and her Sisters are. Now we knew firsthand.

The Sisters themselves often help build new shelters. That fact impressed an Italian news-paperman so much that he paid the Sisters a memorable tribute. His story began:

"We are on the outskirts of Rome near the golf course. To the left . . . there is an unmarked road. Two hundred meters down the road, where the pavement ends, there is a large number of huts and dilapidated shacks.

"The spectacle is incredible! In the midst of several hundred shacks, two masons are constructing a house which looks exactly like all the others. Their helpers are a dozen religious Sisters, seven of them Indian. One of them is the superior of the group. She does the same kind of work as the others.

"The masons are very satisfied with these exceptional helpers. They say they work hard. They are tireless. They never hear a complaint from their lips. These Sisters carry bricks, clay, water, hold the ladder, raise the scaffold with smiles, as if they were always happy. Maybe they are.

"They have been busy with this work all summer. In one month the shack will be finished. And it will be transformed into a convent, school, and hospital. All this in two or three very small rooms.

"I arrived at this scene all splattered with mud. I had to walk the last 300 meters. The taxi driver had refused to go any further, even after I offered him more money. He would not risk his car on such a road.

"The trip had been almost a poetic experience. The Roman taxi driver, in love with his city, had been pointing out the beautiful sights along the way. We had traveled along one of the most famous streets in the entire world, the Via Appia.

"We were no longer on a scenic route when we

approached Tor Fiscale 73, where the first Roman house of the Missionaries of Charity would be. There, on the outskirts of the famed Via Appia, in plain sight of charming Roman villas, you see a large slum consisting of shacks with no plumbing. Children covered with dirt and scarcely dressed, in spite of the cold, were in abundance.

"After walking the last 300 meters on foot, and with great difficulty, I found the Sisters. There was not a shack where they did not know the people and where the people did not know them well. No one called them Missionaries of Charity. Here, everyone called them the *suore indiane,* the Indian Sisters. Above all, they were the friends of the children and the old people who had been abandoned and were sick.

"Their house was little more than a simple shack. It served as convent, school, hospital, and refuge. The walls were not whitewashed. There were light bulbs hanging from uncovered wires — only one in each room, and of low wattage. There were one or two plain chairs, old clothes, and medicines.

"The yard was only a few square meters of space. It had five or six hens crowded in with a few eight-year-old children playing hide-and-seek behind some old sheets and rags that were hanging out to dry. In one room I discovered the almost paralyzed body of an old man curled up on a mattress. A Sister assured me that he was still alive. The impression I had was that he was dead.

"I spoke of Mother Teresa with the superior, an Indian Sister. I also talked about the poor in Rome and in Calcutta, where the superior had worked until she was asked to transfer to Rome.

"I asked her if there was a difference between the poor in India and Rome. She answered, 'You do not see any television antennas coming out of the rooftops in the slums in Calcutta and throughout India as you see them in some shacks here in Rome. But this difference is more apparent than real. In reality, the poor in Rome, like most poor people in the Western hemisphere, are worse off than those in Calcutta or in India. The poor in India believe in something. The poor here in Rome do not seem to believe in anything. That makes them more miserable.'"

One day, a few months after the Sisters arrived in Rome, a high-ranking Vatican official went to see them in a luxurious car. When his car reached a certain point, the road was impassable. The official had to get out of his car and continue on foot.

The only thing that is known about the incident is that the Vatican "spy" who walked into the sea of mud was most impressed by the "Indian Sisters." Before leaving, he offered them his expensive car as a present. The Sisters took it — but not for themselves. They sold it and gave the money to the poor.

This is what the Sisters always do with gifts. The best example is the gift Mother Teresa received from Pope Paul VI in December 1964. The Holy Father had gone to the International Eucharistic Congress in Bombay. Awaiting him there was a new, white Lincoln convertible, donated by Catholics in the United States.

During the Congress, Mother Teresa was also in Bombay to help the poor and to visit her Sisters who have houses there. When she could, Mother

Teresa mingled with the crowds to listen to the Pope. But she was not present when he addressed "crowds, poor and spiritual, avid, packed, naked, attentive crowds that one sees only in India," just before he boarded the plane that took him back to Rome.

Mother Teresa was not present for the Pope's parting words. In the House for the Dying at Chappel Lane 17, old man Onil was struggling with death. That is where Mother Teresa was, at the old man's bedside. So she did not hear the Pope mention her name in his farewell speech at the airport. He not only mentioned her name, he announced that the car he had used in India would be a gift for Mother Teresa "for her universal mission of love."

Neither Mother Teresa nor any of her Sisters ever rode in that car.

They raffled it off. What better way, they thought, to use it as the Pope had suggested, for their "universal mission of love."

A poor widow held the winning ticket. She had hoped to give the car to her son. But the powerful car used so much gas that it was too expensive for him to operate. So the car was sold. The widow kept only half the money for herself. The rest went to Mother Teresa for the poor.

Above: Mother Teresa embraces war orphans in Belfast.

Below: Partial view of *Nirmal Hriday,* the Home for

Above: A common sight on the streets of Calcutta.
the Dying in Calcutta where Mother Teresa works.

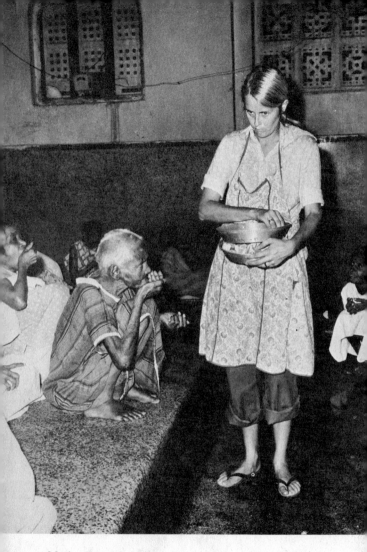

Mother Teresa's example draws people of all backgrounds
and religions to love and serve the poorest of the poor.

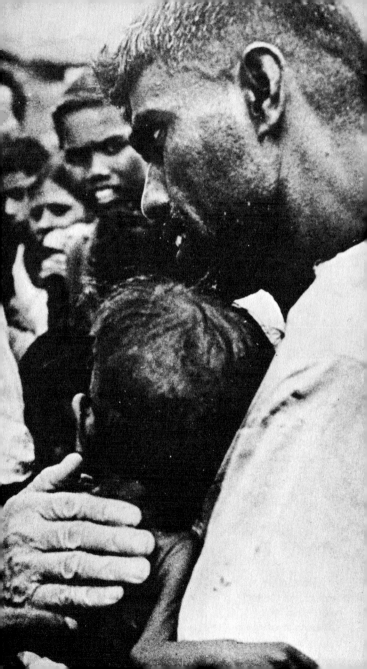

Malcolm Muggeridge
Mère Teresa de Calcutta

aux Éditions du Seuil, Paris

Something
Beautiful
for God

Malcolm
Muggeridge

Malcolm Mugger-idge, the first jour-nalist to ''discover'' Mother Teresa and make her known in the Western world.

The world's influential magazines discover a new face for their covers: Mother Teresa, the ''living saint'' and ''messenger of love and hope.''

EUROPE

DECEMBER 29, 1975

TIME

Messengers
of Love and Hope

Mother
Teresa

LIVING
SAINTS

9
Poor in Spirit,
Poor in Worldly Goods

"Always love each other;
always love our Lady, Holy Poverty."
Saint Francis of Assisi

The incident that moved Mother Teresa to care for the dying is now known worldwide: her discovery of a woman lying among ants and rats in a pile of rubbish. This encounter resulted in the first Home for the Dying, *Nirmal Hriday*.

What you see in *Nirmal Hriday* is impressive. Despite the smell of death that is everywhere, the experience is not all morbid or gloomy.

The rooms and even the hallways are filled with occupied beds. The beds are purposely low to the ground so that if the patients fall from them, they will not injure themselves. Due to the lack of space, the beds are near each other. The Sisters and their helpers can hardly move among them.

On the mattresses are men, women, and children of every age. The Sisters stand in front of a bed, give a shot to ease pain, straighten a head or an arm to make someone more comfortable. They whisper words of comfort, sometimes a prayer. Once in a while the patients have strength enough to smile in gratitude.

The Missionaries of Charity have the good sense not to burden these people with last-minute counseling. The best the Sisters can offer these poor souls, as they leave this sad world, is loving assistance.

One last joy for these suffering people is to see fellow human beings, impelled by a mysterious faith in God, treating them with sincere and unselfish love.

The hostels for the homeless dying are always filled. There are always two or three more people ready to occupy each bed that becomes empty. Beds empty every day, but more people keep arriving. Some die on their way to the hospital.

There is one essential condition for being accepted in the homes for the dying: the Sisters take in only those who are not accepted in other hospitals or centers. This restriction is due not to discrimination, but to lack of space.

The hostels are always full because the Missionaries of Charity have the help of others in filling them. Their work is so well known that when people discover abandoned persons who are gravely ill, they rush them to Mother Teresa's.

Each day, of course, the Sisters go out on their rounds, looking for suffering. A "search" ambulance also goes out daily. It is not unusual to see Mother Teresa herself traveling in the ambulance looking in areas where human cargo is almost guaranteed.

In Calcutta's *Nirmal Hriday* or in any of the more than 30 other hostels Mother Teresa has opened in India and other countries the dying are offered hygienic care and food. For the first time in their lives, many of them find people who are willing to bathe their diseased flesh, dress their wounds, and offer them a bed.

An old man who had never slept on a mattress caressed the edges of his pallet when he was moved to the hospital. He whispered: "At last I'll be able to lie on a real bed, even if it is to die."

The care that the Missionaries of Charity lavish on the dying cannot prevent most patients from losing their slim grip on life. Seventy to eighty percent soon die, sometimes without ever waking from the unconscious state in which they are found. But some of them do get better. Those who respond and grow stronger are sheltered and given work to do, if they are equal to it. Those who never regain strength are surrounded by love and human warmth. The majority of those who get well can hardly wait to get back on the streets.

Many return again to Mother Teresa, when they see that they can no longer make it alone. They return inspired by the memory of the only place they were ever treated as human beings.

India, more than most other places on earth, is an area abounding in people who need help because of leprosy.

Mother Teresa says, "I know that when I touch the limbs of a leper who stinks, I am touching the body of Christ the same as when I receive his sacramental body in the Eucharist. This conviction of touching Christ under the appearance of a leper gives me a courage which I would not have otherwise."

With this same human concern, all of the Sisters care for society's rejects — and these poor souls abound in India more than anywhere else in the world.

Only 35,000 people — a very small percentage compared to the many untouchables in India — benefit from the Sisters' care. This number takes into account those who enjoy permanent, continuous aid. But the Missionaries of Charity also support mobile dispensaries that help an even larger number of people virtually impossible to estimate.

In any case, the lepers are the Sisters' highest priority. People run from lepers because of an exaggerated fear of contagion. True, there are some incurable cases of leprosy. But there are many more cases today that can be cured — and many more in which the disease and the risk of contagion can be checked. One of the Sisters' greatest frustrations is that they are often deprived of the paltry monthly sum of money needed for the medicines to arrest or cure leprosy.

There are leper couples whose small children have not contracted leprosy. But the children are condemned to it for lack of means to prevent contagion.

Someone once suggested a possible solution to Mother Teresa. "Wouldn't it be best to separate threatened children from their parents?"

She replied: "How are human beings, deprived of everything by their sickness, to be deprived of the warmth of their children?

"How are innocent children to be deprived of loving parents who, because of unfortunate conditions, are more loving and tender with them?"

The easiest solution is one that, unfortunately, is not often applied: treatment of parents and children so that they are rendered noninfectious. Medicines for such treatment cost less than the small baubles that are frequently given to these same children.

Because medicine is not always available, the lepers abound on the outskirts of the city. There they neither annoy others nor threaten contagion. But this situation virtually condemns them to death while still alive. To appease their hunger, they search as well as they can among the garbage dumps. Very often they lack the strength to forage for food scraps. Very often they lose even the will to live.

The lepers run from rejection and persecution by those who are healthy. The ones from the north escape to the south; those from the south escape to the north. They know it is useless to look for work or for any betterment of their existence. They not only run from strangers but from their own loved ones — children from parents, brothers from brothers.

The hopelessness of their situation is what makes lepers the favorites of Mother Teresa and her Sisters. Several of the Sisters specialize in their cure. They take loving care of them, without fear of contagion.

The Sisters also have specialized clinics. They have built an entire town for the lepers, a *Shanti Nagar* — City of Peace — on the outskirts of Calcutta. Here, there is room for 500 families. The land was donated by the Indian government. The money needed to start construction came when Mother Teresa raffled off the white convertible she received from Pope Paul VI.

This is a self-sufficient town, expanding constantly. Its inhabitants have learned to make bricks, do carpentry, print, weave baskets, make shoes, and raise rice and wheat.

All of these tasks serve a useful purpose. But what is even more important is the lepers' tremendous sense of pride in doing things for themselves and others. They regain a sense of usefulness and of belonging.

That is an important thing to Mother Teresa. She wants to keep her Sisters from becoming bureaucrats of charity, simply dispensing the gifts of others to the poor. She wants each Sister to have a strong personal commitment in the work of the order. Each Missionary of Charity must dedicate at least part of her time daily to the physical care of the poorest of the poor.

Mother Teresa leads the way. She pulls up her sleeves, washes dishes, cleans the convent toilet, salves and bandages wounds, washes the dirty and smelly bodies of lepers. On the day Mother Teresa went to the Vatican to receive the John XXIII International Peace Prize from the hands of the pope himself, she helped the other Sisters do these same chores right up till the moment she left.

Mother Teresa lives her own philosophy: "Our best protection is in our poverty."

It is a material poverty, symbolic of a spiritual poverty which consists of always being available for others, going at anytime, anywhere, to serve Christ in the distressed people who cry out for help.

As one Missionary of Charity put it: "I am in Calcutta, but I am not settled down nor will I settle down anywhere. I prefer to be like a Bohemian, going from one place of work to another until I die." She assured me that half an hour after receiving an order to move, she is already on the train to her new destination.

"We could not understand and effectively help those who lack everything if we didn't live like them," says Mother Teresa. "The difference between the poverty of the poorest of the poor and our poverty is that they have been forced into poverty, and we are poor by choice. If we weren't deeply convinced that Christ remains hidden in the face of the disowned of this world, our life would be impossible."

The poverty of the Missionaries of Charity is a very visible poverty, set against a background of total serenity. They are quite happy with just a few personal belongings. Each Sister has two blue-edged, white *saris*, made out of the cheapest cotton and worth only $1.00 each, a pair of sandals, a crucifix, a rosary, a basin to wash in, and a very narrow mattress made of straw for a few hours rest each night. They try to get by with as few things as the poor they serve. Each Sister lives in a state of personal poverty. So does each community and the entire order.

Naturally, the poverty of the Missionaries of Charity is not an end in itself. They are poor not for the sake of being poor, but to meet the poor on their own level — to show that their love is genuine.

In order to be more effective in their work, the Sisters learn occupations and professions. They become nurses and social workers. They study medicine and law. But the level of professional competence achieved does not bring any rank or privilege to the Sisters. They all perform any of the services needed by their patients.

These Sisters are not only poor in spirit, they are also poor in worldly goods.

10
An Avalanche of Awards

"All of us are but God's instruments,
who do our little bit and pass by."
Mother Teresa

The religious life is a series of paradoxes.

No one knows this better than Mother Teresa. She has never sought the limelight nor awards for herself. Yet, the more she protests her unworthiness, the more she is showered with honors.

She received her first public recognition in 1962. The president of the Indian Federation, with Prime Minister Pandit Nehru attending, presented her with the *Padma Shri* (Lotus Order), a high award given by the government of India.

In Manila the following year, the Conference of Asiatic States awarded her the Magsaysay Prize, proclaiming her "the most worthy woman in Asia."

In 1965 her order won a rare distinction: Pope Paul VI named it a Pontifical Congregation.

In 1970 she received two prizes in the United States — the Good Samaritan Prize and that of the Kennedy Foundation, which was given in recognition of "her love and selfless devotion to the physically and emotionally handicapped, as well as to the masses of the disowned of the entire world."

In 1972 she became the first to receive the Pandit Nehru Award for International Understanding as recognition for "her generous service, without prejudice due to nationality, race or religion, and without looking for public reward or recognition on anyone's part.''

Mother Teresa received two more awards in 1973, the Templeton Prize in London and the Saint Louise de Marillac in Los Angeles. She has also received the gold medallion of the city of Milan, Italy, and the designation, Mother of Asia.

In 1975 she received the Albert Schweitzer Award in the United States. In that same year the FAO (the United Nations organization for nutrition) minted a medallion which bears Mother Teresa's face and is sold to benefit her work.

In 1979 she received the Balzan Award, given to her personally by the President of the Italian Republic, Sandro Pertini. This award has been given previously to Pope John XXIII.

That same year, Mother Teresa received the Nobel Peace Prize.

This is a most impressive list — but not to Mother Teresa. The story goes that when she received the £34,000 Templeton Prize, she was about to leave when she was asked, "Where is the prize?" She had forgotten to bring it. Someone later found it on a chair and returned it to her.

A month before his death Pope John XXIII received the Balzan Prize for Humanity, Peace, and Brotherhood. With it he received a check for $300,000. At the time, John XXIII was close to death. His wish for this money was that it go to a suitable cause. He therefore instituted a new award in his name.

The first time the award was given, the jury unanimously selected Mother Teresa of Calcutta for the honor. She was praised for "the exceptional abnegation with which she has dedicated her whole life in aiding, in India and other countries of the world, the victims of hunger, misery, and illness, the abandoned and the dying, transforming into tireless action her love for suffering humanity.''

The award was given to Mother by Pope Paul VI in a solemn ceremony at the Vatican. The whole diplomatic corps accredited by the Holy See was present, along with fifteen princes of the Church, many monsignors, and other Church dignitaries.

Meanwhile, Mother Teresa, the guest of honor, came by streetcar. She was dressed in her $1.00 Indian *sari*.

Pope Paul VI, one of Mother Teresa's most devoted admirers, spoke feelingly of that ''humble and quiet, but not unknown religious, Mother Teresa, who has been developing a wonderful mission of love for the last twenty years in India in favor of the lepers, old people, and abandoned children.'' He concluded: ''We propose to all the admiration of this intrepid messenger of Christ's love.''

The first time that the prestigious Templeton Prize for Progress in Religion was given, the jury chose Mother Teresa among 2,000 proposed candidates. The jury was composed of ten people, all members of different religious denominations: two Anglicans, two Presbyterians, one Methodist, one Jew, one Muslim, one Buddhist monk, one Hindu, and one Catholic.

On accepting the award, Mother Teresa said, ''In giving this award to me, actually it is given to the people, to all those who share with me throughout the world in the work of love, in spreading God's love amongst men.

"Actually we are touching His body. It is the hungry Christ that we are feeding, it is the naked Christ that we are clothing, it is the homeless Christ that we are giving shelter and it is not just hunger for bread, and nakedness for cloth, and homelessness for a house made of bricks but Christ today is hungry in our poor people, and even in the rich, for love, for being cared for, for being wanted, for having someone to call their own.

"Here in England, and in other places such as Calcutta, we find lonely people who are known by the number of their room. Where are we then? Do we really know that there are some people, maybe next door to us? Maybe there is a blind man who would be happy if you would read the newspaper for him. Maybe there is a rich person who has no one to visit him. He has plenty of other things but he is nearly drowned in them. There is no touch; and he needs your touch. Some time back, a very rich man came to our place and he told me: this I give you for somebody to come to my house. I am nearly half blind, and my wife is nearly mental, and our children have all gone abroad. And we are dying of loneliness. They are longing for the loving sound of a human voice.

"And here in this city — great city — of London, there is so much — so much that you and I can do. The first time I was here in London, we went out at night. It was a terrible, cold night and we found the people on the street. And there was an old man, well-spoken man, shivering with cold. He was in front of me. In front of him there was another old man — a black man — with his coat open. He was protecting him from the cold.

"This gentleman was saying 'Take me, take me anywhere, I am longing to sleep between two sheets.' He was a well-spoken man and must have had better days. But there he was. And we looked around and we could see many. Not as many as in Calcutta. not as many, maybe as in other places, but here there are many. If there is just one, he is Jesus, he is the one that is hungry for love, for care. And as it is written in the Scripture 'I looked for one to care for me and I couldn't find him.' How terrible it would be if Jesus had to say that to us today, after dying for us on the cross."

Receiving awards and attending world functions, by now, has become such a demanding part of Mother Teresa's schedule that she announced on April 1, 1980, that she will no longer participate in ceremonies honoring her. "The public gaze that has fallen on me after I received the Nobel Prize is hindering normal works of service to the poor."

Therefore, let us focus our spotlight for a moment on the one man who has contributed the most to making her work known: Malcolm Muggeridge, the English newsman and author.

He took a BBC team to Calcutta in the spring of 1969 to do a film about Mother Teresa and her work. He was an agnostic, despite his friendship with the Catholic Primate of England at that time, Cardinal Heenan. But Malcolm Muggeridge quickly became an admirer of Mother Teresa. In the book he wrote about her, *Something Beautiful for God,* he wrote: "I never met anyone so memorable. She is a burning and shining light; in a cruel time, a living embodiment of Christ's gospel of love; in a godless time, the Word dwelling among us, full of grace and truth."

A remarkable thing happened during the filming of the documentary *Something Beautiful for God*. One particular sequence was taken in a dark, cavernous building, *Nirmal Hriday,* where the Sisters bring the dying. The sequence was expected to be unusable because of the poor light. To the astonishment of the entire crew, the scene came out bathed in an exquisite light. Muggeridge commented: "Some of Mother Teresa's light had got into it."

This simple, filmed portrait of Mother Teresa and her Sisters at work often focused on the most miserable scenes. But it had a tremendous impact. In spite of the fact that there was not a single request for donations, money poured in the moment the documentary was shown on TV. £ 20,000 came in the mails in a few weeks!

Later, the documentary film was shown to American, French, German, Italian, and Dutch viewers as well as to the British. If millions of people today know of Mother Teresa's work, they owe this knowledge mainly to Malcolm Muggeridge. His televised documentary and his book about Mother Teresa have been the greatest factors in making her well known in the West.

As one researcher who has collected much data from the work of Malcolm Muggeridge, I confess my admiration and gratitude to this old lion of British journalism.

11
How Others Share
Mother Teresa's Work

"Don't ever allow anyone,
especially your own,
to feel lonely, unwanted or unloved."
Mother Teresa

Mother Teresa tries to arrange a spiritual partnership between each of her communities and an outside religious contemplative community. This form of spiritual union has been welcomed with great enthusiasm.

A great number of cloistered monasteries in many countries have adopted Mother's idea. Each monastery, or group of contemplatives consecrated to God, has agreed to share in Mother Teresa's work by offering their prayers for one of her communities.

In addition to these religious communities, there are many individual lay persons whose spiritual generosity should be noted. Jacqueline de Decker is one name now linked with that of Mother Teresa.

They met in Patna, India, in 1949. After leaving the Loreto Sisters, Sister Teresa had decided to take a brief nursing course before starting her new work. At the center where Sister Teresa studied nursing, a lay Belgian missionary, Jacqueline de Decker, was recuperating from a grave illness.

The one woman, Sister Teresa, was about to undertake a difficult life. The other was on the verge of mandatory retirement due to the loss of her health. They became friends.

Jacqueline de Decker left India and returned to Belgium to undergo several operations on her spine. The surgery failed to improve her condition. Accustomed to working generously for others, Jacqueline now foresaw a useless life ahead of her.

Mother Teresa, however, convinced her dear friend that this did not have to be. She made an immediate proposal: Why not begin a close association, with Jacqueline using her prayers and sacrifices to be a spiritual godmother to Mother Teresa? Jacqueline agreed at once, delighted to have this new horizon of hope opened to her.

Every day since that time, Jacqueline has offered her prayers for all the Missionaries of Charity.

One day, Jacqueline received a letter from Mother Teresa which read:

"You and others who unite with you will share in our prayers, our work, and all our undertakings. With your sufferings you will share in all we are able to do. The purpose of our congregation is to quench Jesus' thirst for people's love. We do this by working for the good of the people in the slums. But who could do it better than you and others who suffer and are sick? What you can do from your bed of pain has more value than what I can do with my hurried trips among the crowded poor. But, together, you and I are capable of all in Him who is our strength."

Jacqueline was the first and later the head of all the "Sick and Suffering Co-Workers" of the

Missionaries of Charity. They exist now in many countries.

Jacqueline de Decker's body is 90 percent paralyzed. Yet, she testifies that she is happy in her suffering because of the meaning that her role of Co-Worker and spiritual support for Mother Teresa has given her.

Many more people in England, France, the United States, Spain, Canada, Germany, Belgium, Poland, Hungary, Holland, and Italy who are ill now feel that same happiness.

Mother Teresa shares their joy. In another letter to Jacqueline she says:

"All of you are a particular cause of happiness for me. When the work is hardest, I often think about each one of you and, in consideration of your sufferings, I ask God to bless our efforts. I have the feeling God always listens to me right away . . . ."

Invalids have a special place in the association headed by Jacqueline de Decker. But Mother Teresa invites all who are sick and suffering to join in her prayers. "All who wish to enter the association are entirely welcome. But the favorites are the paralyzed, the handicapped, all who are incurably ill."

At this writing, thousands of Sick and Suffering Co-Workers have already "adopted a Sister or Brother." No exact count is made of those who join, because the numbers change from one day to the next. Nevertheless, the number of Sick and Suffering Co-Workers who have a silent, spiritual sharing in Mother Teresa's work is a remarkable phenomenon. Prayers flood in daily from all over the world.

Mother Teresa's way of life is one of dedication. But it is a life anyone can live. Speaking to family people, Mother emphasizes that love begins at home. She writes:

"I want so much for you as Co-Workers to make your homes another Nazareth where peace, love, joy and happiness reign. You are Co-Workers of Jesus and being His Co-Workers you are touching Him, you are loving Him in your own family, for love must begin at home. You have a mission to fulfill, a mission of love, but this must begin in your own homes. You must have time for your own first, and after that your works for others. Make your homes centers of compassion and forgive endlessly. Be kind and merciful. Let no one ever come to you without coming away better and happier. Let us begin, then, in the place where we are, with the people with whom we are the closest, and then spread out.

"Fidelity to small acts will help us to grow in love. We have all been given a lighted lamp and it is for us to keep it burning. We can keep it burning only if we keep on pouring oil inside. That oil comes from those acts of love. So let us keep that lamp burning, so when He comes He will know us. He will know not only you and me, but all those people we have come in contact with. He will find Himself in all of them, because of the love they have received and the love they have given."

In a Co-Worker newsletter, a mother of five small children shared her insight into life as a Co-Worker. This woman's experience applies just as well to people who take care of their parents or family members of any age. She writes:

"Many times when I read in the newsletter all of

the inspiring works other Co-Workers are doing I think, 'Oh, I'd better get going and do much more. I'm sloughing off.' And so for awhile I try visiting nursing homes or some other good endeavor to make *me* feel better. Just recently, though, I have come to a startling awareness. I call it a gift of grace from Jesus.

"Since I have five small children and a busy and dedicated husband, my priorities for now must begin and end right here in our home. Mother Teresa has said this many times in her words to all kinds of groups. But never have I realized as now the depth of those words — 'to bring Jesus first in the home.'

"Having just read the two new books about Mother Teresa, *To Give the Love of Jesus,* by James McGovern, and *Servant of Love,* by Father Edward Le Joly, I am now trying to incorporate the three things Mother stresses in both books. These are: (1) Complete Surrender, (2) Complete Trust and (3) Cheerfulness.

"In my 'work' as a wife and mother, these are very essential. I must surrender to Christ *through* complete surrender to my family. To be there to serve them in their needs — to establish a 'house of charity' in our home.

"In serving my family I must strive to be cheerful so that I can adequately reflect Jesus' love for my family and thus help them to want to know, love and serve Him.

"I must then trust Him completely, knowing that each day He will give me the measure of love and patience I will need.

"Absurd and ironic as it may seem, to work for my family is considered at this time in the U.S.A.

to be the lowliest of endeavors— and so all the more appropriate for a Co-Worker.

"In embracing my family in this way I know that Jesus will not waste my efforts and I will become a better instrument which He can use. As this part of my life progresses and the children become more independent, He may then see fit to trust me to serve Him in other ways. But mostly I will know, please God, that six people will have had a look at Jesus' love for them and then they perhaps will influence others to love Him too."

In the United States in the late 1950s, the National Council of Catholic Women began to support the work of Mother Teresa through annual contributions to a "Madonna Plan" fund. The fund was administered by Catholic Relief Services (CRS), the overseas relief agency of the Catholic Church in the U.S. As CRS reported its use of the funds to Catholic women in the United States, the work of Mother Teresa became more widely known. Eileen Egan, the CRS Project Supervisor for India and a longtime friend of Mother Teresa, served as liaison between CRS and the Council of Catholic Women. Two early supporters of Mother Teresa's work were the diocesan Councils of Catholic Women in Brooklyn, New York, and Peoria, Illinois.

In the late 1950s and through the 1960s, articles about Mother Teresa's life and work appeared ever more frequently in magazines and newspapers throughout the world. A book and a documentary film by Malcolm Muggeridge, both entitled *Something Beautiful for God,* generated considerable interest in the early 1970s.

Inquiries about the work of Mother Teresa

began to flow to Calcutta, to CRS, and to people associated with Mother. It soon became apparent that a more orderly line of communication was needed. So Mother Teresa began a loose-knit international organization of individuals who could advise and encourage those who wished to help the Missionaries of Charity through prayer and service.

Out of these individuals and groups grew the International Association of Co-Workers of Mother Teresa. Mother Teresa presented the Constitution of the Association to Pope Paul VI. With his blessing, the International Association of Co-Workers of Mother Teresa became affiliated with the Missionaries of Charity on March 29, 1969.

A national chairman was appointed for each country under the leadership of the International Link, Mrs. Ann Blaikie of England. In 1955, while living with her family in Calcutta, Ann Blaikie had been one of the first volunteers to join in the work.

Mrs. Patricia Kump of Minneapolis, Minnesota, who had been guiding the American Co-Workers under Mother Teresa's direction since 1959, was named Chairman of the American Branch of the International Association of Co-Workers.

The Association of Co-Workers is as innovative as the rest of Mother Teresa's ideas. One doesn't "join," pay a fee, or get a membership card. Belonging is above all an inner gesture, a spiritual commitment. Mother Teresa calls it a "way of life." This way of life, as well as advice on how one may become her Co-Worker, is described in the following leaflet which has been circulated all over the world:

The Co-Worker's Way of Life

*The Co-Worker's Way of Life
is a Way of Love.*

1. The International Association of "Co-Workers of Mother Teresa" consists of men, women, young people, and children of all religions and denominations throughout the world, who seek to love God in their fellowmen through wholehearted free service to the poorest of the poor of all castes and creeds, and who wish to unite their lives in the spirit of prayer and sacrifice with the work of Mother Teresa and the Missionaries of Charity.

2. The aim of the International Association is to help its members:
   • To recognize God in the person of the poor and to love Him better through works of charity and service to the poor.
   • To know the poor. Knowledge leads to love, and love to service. And so all Co-Workers should give their hearts to love them and their hands to serve them.
   • To radiate love and compassion in their homes, communities, and their surroundings.
   • To form, where possible, communities of Co-Workers desirous of sharing more deeply in the life of sacrifice and work of the Missionaries of Charity.

3. The "poorest of the poor" are the hungry, the thirsty, the naked, the homeless, the ignorant, the captives, the crippled, the leprosy sufferers, the alcoholics and drug addicts, the dying destitutes and the bereaved, the unloved, the

abandoned, the outcasts and all those who have lost all hope and faith in life.

4. The Co-Workers recognize the dignity, the individuality and the infinite value of every human life.

5. Christ, being rich, became poor for love of us, and since we are trying to live a life of love in action, we too should free ourselves from all that is binding and love one another as He loves us.

6. At the same time and in the same spirit, Co-Workers make available to the Missionaries of Charity whatever time and material and spiritual help are within their power to provide, and offer their God-given talents in the service of the poor.

7. As the Missionaries of Charity give wholehearted free service to the poor, so do the Co-Workers with love and joy.

8. The Sick and Suffering Co-Workers and those unable to join in activities may become linked with an individual Sister or Brother by offering their prayers and suffering for such a Brother or Sister, and supported where possible by the Co-Workers.

9. Contemplative Orders may be linked in prayer with Communities of the Missionaries of Charity.

10. The Co-Workers of Mother Teresa are not a fund-raising organization. Mother Teresa only accepts voluntary and unsolicited gifts (those given from the heart). ALL money donated for the Missionaries of Charity and sent to the Treasurer of the Co-Workers will be forwarded in its entirety to the Mis-

sionaries of Charity to be used according to the intentions of the donors for the poor served by the Missionaries of Charity.

Life of Prayer

1. Let us learn to pray the work by doing it in His presence; by doing it with Him, for Him and to Him all the 24 hours.
2. Co-Workers of Mother Teresa unite with the Missionaries of Charity by praying the daily prayer (see below).
3. Co-Workers should be encouraged to have one hour of prayer and meditation together at least once a month.
4. An Annual Day of Prayer and Thanksgiving will be held on October 7th throughout the world, being the day on which the Society of the Missionaries of Charity was founded in 1950. On that day all are asked to unite with the Sisters and Brothers in giving thanks to God.

Life of Love in Action

1. All Co-Workers express their love of God through service to the poor as Jesus Christ Himself has said: "Whatever you did to the least of these My brethren, you did it to Me" (Matthew 25:40). "For I was hungry and you gave Me to eat, I was thirsty and you gave Me to drink. I was homeless and you took Me in, naked and you clothed Me, in prison and you came to see Me" (Matthew 25:35).
2. In answer to Christ's plea to love one another as He has loved us, Co-Workers should become sensitive and responsive to the needs of their family, their next-door neighbor, those

in their street, in their town, their country, and the whole world. Co-Workers, by putting their understanding love into action, no matter how small the action may be, will thus share in the "wholehearted free service to the poor" which the Sisters and Brothers vow to God.

3. Informal Communities of Co-Workers, by their understanding love for one another, their joyful spirit and life of love and service, will show forth in their neighborhoods the way to peace and joy.

4. The keynotes of the giving are Love and Service.

What Is a Co-Worker?

A Co-Worker of Mother Teresa is one who chooses a way of life that calls for seeing God in every human being. In seeing God in everyone, starting with those closest to us, we become ready to share ourselves with the lonely, the ill, the bereaved, the poor and the unwanted. We are strengthened by being part of a worldwide company of those who bear witness to the presence of God in every member of the family of man.

How Does One Become a Co-Worker?

We become a Co-Worker simply by wanting to be one. It is not an "organization" in the ordinary sense of the word, but rather a family whose members seek to come closer to God and to each other through prayer and loving service to their fellowmen. Mother Teresa keeps in touch with her Co-Workers through Newsletters which are circulated among Co-Workers.

How May One Serve as an Active Co-Worker?

Mother Teresa desires her Co-Workers to maintain deep family love in the home, and beyond that, to seek to serve those in need in their own neighborhood, their town, their country, the world. Mother Teresa asks that we find *those who need us* and get to know them personally. She tells us: *We must go to those who have no one, to those who suffer from the worst disease of all, the disease of being unwanted, unloved, uncared for.*

Mother Teresa reminds her Co-Workers that *it is only when we know the people that we can understand and love them.* She asks the Co-Workers to do the "little things," the things no one else has time for. Thus many Co-Workers have formed loving relationships with those in hospitals, nursing homes, prisons, and homes for the physically and mentally handicapped, with the bereaved or with the elderly who wait day after lonely day for the compassionate touch of a friend.

At Mother Teresa's suggestion Co-Workers come together regularly for one hour of prayer and meditation. She says: *You will come closer to God, to each other and to the people through this hour.* And so across the world, informal communities of Co-Workers, young and old, rich and poor, able and disabled meet for this hour with God and with each other.

The Co-Workers' Prayer

MAKE US worthy, Lord, to serve our fellowmen throughout the world who live and die in poverty and hunger.

GIVE THEM, through our hands, this day their daily bread; and by our understanding love, give peace and joy.

LORD, make me a channel of Thy peace,
that where there is hatred, I may bring love;
that where there is wrong,
    I may bring the spirit of forgiveness;
that where there is discord,
    I may bring harmony;
that where there is error, I may bring truth;
that where there is doubt, I may bring faith;
that where there is despair, I may bring hope;
that where there are shadows,
    I may bring light;
that where there is sadness, I may bring joy.

LORD, grant that I may seek rather to comfort than to be comforted; to understand than to be understood; to love than to be loved; for it is by forgetting self that one finds; it is by forgiving that one is forgiven; it is by dying that one awakens to eternal life. Amen.

Those interested in knowing more about the active, contemplative, or Sick and Suffering Co-Workers in the United States may write to the Chairman of the American Co-Workers of Mother Teresa:

Mrs. Vi Collins
5106 Battery Lane
Bethesda, Maryland 20814

12
Mother Teresa's Message of Love

The First Sisters
One by one, since 1949, I saw young girls arriving. They had been my students. They wanted to give everything to God, and they were in a hurry to do it. They took off their expensive *saris* with great satisfaction in order to put on our humble cotton *sari*. They came fully aware that this was a very difficult thing. When a girl who belongs to a very old caste comes to place herself at the service of the outcasts, we are talking about a revolution. The biggest one. The hardest of all: the revolution of love!   M.T.

Christ's Face
Our first task consists of washing faces and bodies. The majority of the people don't know what soap is and lather frightens them. If the Sisters were not able to discover Christ's face in these unfortunate people, their work would be impossible.   M.T.

Human Dignity
We are concerned that they come to realize there are those who offer them a sincere love. Here they find their human dignity once more and they die in the midst of an impressive silence . . . God loves silence.   M.T.

We Offer Joy to the Poor
The poor deserve not only to be served; they also deserve happiness. The Sisters try to offer it to them in abundance.   M.T.

My Faith and My Life

I would be willing to give up my life, but not my faith.   M.T.

Who Is Our Neighbor?

The people in whose search we must go can live far or near. They can be materially or spiritually poor. They can hunger for peace or for love. They can lack clothing or the knowledge of the richness of God's love for them. They can be searching for a shelter made of bricks and cement or for a house made with the love in our heart.   M.T.

What Counts Is Love

We don't have to do great things to show great love for God and neighbor. It is the love we put into our actions which makes our offering something beautiful for God.   M.T.

Loving God in Others

Our work is nothing more than the expression of our love for God. We have to shower our love on someone, and the people are our means of expressing our love for God.   M.T.

Waste Makes Me Angry

There must be a reason that some people are able to live comfortably. Perhaps they have achieved this through their work. I get angry only when I see waste, when I see people throwing away things we could use for the poor.   M.T.

Jesus Comes

Today, once more, Jesus comes among His own and His own do not know Him. He comes in the hurt bodies of our poor. But He even comes in the rich who abound with riches. He comes in the loneliness of their hearts, when there is no one who loves them. Jesus comes to you and me. And often, very often, we let Him pass without noticing Him.   M.T.

Christ Is in the Poor

Let us never forget that in the service of the poor, an opportunity is offered to us to do something beautiful for God. Because, when we give ourselves fully to the free service of the poor, we really offer it to Christ in His distressing disguise, as He Himself said: *You have done it for me.* . . .   M.T.

The Smile When Taking and Giving

When a poor person comes to you, receive him or her with a smile. This is the greatest gift God has given you: having the strength to accept anything he might give you and being willing to give back to him anything he might ask of you.   M.T.

Heaven from Here

We all long for heaven where God is, but we are all offered the opportunity to be in heaven with God starting right now and to be happy with Him at this very moment. Being happy with God means loving as He loves, helping as He helps, giving as He gives, serving as He serves, saving as He saves, being with Him twenty-four hours a day in touch with His suffering image in the *poorest* of the poor.   M.T.

Life Is a Gift from God

Christ has said that we are more important in His Father's eyes than the grass, the birds, and the flowers of the fields. Therefore, if He takes care of these things, much more care will He take of His life in us. He cannot deceive us, because life is God's greatest gift to human beings who, as far as being created in His image, belong to Him. We don't have any right to destroy it.   M.T.

Life Is Sacred

I do not affirm whether abortion should be or not be legal. I believe that no human hand should be raised to end life. All life is God's life in us. And even an unborn child has God's life in him or her. We have no right whatsoever to destroy such a life, whatever the ways might be to do so. Man, woman, or child: There is no difference. It seems to me that a cry from those unborn children is reaching us, children who are murdered before coming into this world — a cry that echoes before God's throne.   M.T.

A Beautiful Experience

The poor, the lepers, the dispossessed, the neglected, and even the alcoholics we serve are all great people. Many of them have extraordinary personalities. We should communicate this experience, which comes from serving them, to those who do not have or have never had such a beautiful possibility. It is one of the greatest comforts in our work.   M.T.

A Human Voice

There are people who long for the kind sound of a human voice.   M.T.

Forgiveness and Peace

The Christian has to learn to forgive. We have to realize that in order to be forgiven, we have to be able to forgive. I am thinking about Northern Ireland, Bangladesh, Amman and other places: only if they succeed in forgiving will they have peace.   M.T.

People and Structures

If anyone feels that God wants him or her to change the structures in society, that is a matter between God and that person. We all have the duty to serve God where we feel called. I feel called to help individuals, to love each person, not to interest myself in institutions. I do not feel like judging and condemning.   M.T.

Love and Money

I try to give to the poor with love what the rich get with money. It is true: I would not touch a leper for a million dollars. But I cure their wounds for the love of Christ.   M.T.

Loving Those We Have Near

It is easy to love those who are far. It isn't always easy to love those who are right next to us. It is easier to offer a dish of rice to satisfy the hunger of a poor person than to fill up the loneliness and suffering of someone lacking love in our own family.   M.T.

The Worst Misfortune

We must look for those who need us the most. Look for those who don't have anyone, those who suffer the worst misfortune: that of not having

anyone who worries about them, who loves them,
who cares for them.   M.T.

We Will Be Judged on Love

We will be judged according to how we have
treated the hungry, the sick, the marginated. We
will be judged on the love we have shown them.
They are our hope, our guarantee of salvation. We
should get closer to each one of them and treat
them as we would treat Jesus himself. It makes no
difference who they are: we must see God in
them.   M.T.

Christ in the Neglected

Christ is present today in the people who are
considered unwanted, who have no job, who do
not receive any attention or care, who are hungry,
who have no clothing or shelter. The state and
society consider them parasites. No one has time
for them. You and I are worthy, as Christians, of
Christ's love if our love is real. We have the duty
of looking for these people and helping them.
They are there so we can go to meet them. M.T.

The Neighbor Across the Street

We come across people who are only known by
their address number. Do we really realize that
such people exist? Perhaps across the street. It
might be a blind person who would be happy if we
volunteered to read the newspaper. It might even
be someone rich who has no one to visit. The rich
person has a lot of things, but he is smothered by
them. He lacks human contact and that is what
that person needs.   M.T.

Instruments

We are merely instruments who do our small part and disappear. M.T.

Finding God in Silence

We need to find God and God cannot be found in the noise and uproar. God is a friend of silence. M.T.

Death of the Poor

We contemplate death every day. It is beautiful to see these people die with such dignity, radiating happiness because they are going back to where they came from, returning to the only one who loves them. Those who own many things, who own abundant goods and riches, are obsessed with them. They think that what counts the most are riches. That is why they find it hard to leave everything. This is much easier for the poor who are so free because their freedom allows them to leave happy. M.T.

Dignity of the Poor

The poor are good people. They have their own dignity which we can appreciate. Generally, the poor are not known and that is why people are not able to see their dignity. But they have great courage to live the life they live. They are forced to live that way. We welcome our poverty. They are forced to accept it. M.T.

Unknown Greatness

People don't know they have lost their faith. If they were convinced that the person lying in the dirt is their brother or sister, I believe they would do something for that person. People don't know what compassion is. They don't know people. If they understood, they would immediately realize the greatness of the people lying in the street and would simply love them. And the love would surely lead them to place themselves at their service.   M.T.

My Spiritual Food

The Mass is the spiritual food that nourishes me. Without it I would not be able to survive one day nor one hour of my life. Jesus comes to us under the appearance of bread at Mass, while in the slums we see Christ and touch him in the broken bodies and the abandoned children. M.T.

The Crowd and the Person

I never think in terms of a crowd, only of one person. If I visualized a crowd, I would never get started. What matters is the individual person. I believe in the meeting of persons.   M.T.

The Present in India

India needs technicians, scientists, economists, doctors, and hygienists for its development. It needs plans and needs a coordinated general action. But how long will people have to wait so that such plans produce their effects? We don't know. In the meantime, people need to live. They have to be fed, taken care of, dressed. Our area of work is India's present. As long as the present lasts, our work continues to be useful and necessary.   M.T.

My Poor

My community are the poor. Their security is my own. Their heart is my own. My house is the house of the poor — not just of the poor, but of the *poorest* of the poor: those who are so dirty and full of contagious germs that no one goes near them; those who do not go to pray because they are naked; those who do not eat because they do not have the strength; those who collapse on the sidewalks, knowing they are about to die, while the living walk by them without even looking back; those who do not cry because they have no more tears left. M.T.

Providence Helps Us

We depend solely on divine providence. Christ has said that we are more important in His eyes than the flowers, the grass, and the birds. He takes care of our people. We take care of thousands of people in India and other places, and up to now we have always had something. We have never had the need to reject anyone for lack of space or food. God has always been present with His love and solicitude. M.T.

Death Is a Return Home

After all, death is nothing but the easiest and fastest way to return to God. If only we could believe, if we could make people understand that we come from God and we have to return to Him! Each person knows that we have not created ourselves. Someone, another, has given us life. To return to Him is to return home. M.T.

Resources: Film and Cassette Tapes

The World of Mother Teresa is a marvelous film showing Mother at work with her people in India. By capturing Mother Teresa's great humanness and sense of humor, this film evokes a desire to serve the Lord with joy. Available as of January 1981, this 58-minute 16mm color film can be purchased or rented by contacting Ann Petrie Productions, 225 W. 106 Street, New York, NY 10025.

The four tapes listed here are useful for shut-ins, students, Co-Worker gatherings, and all who wish to hear the message of Mother Teresa.

To obtain the two following tapes, send cash or check payable to Mrs. Sandra A. McMurtrie, 9103 North Branch Drive, Bethesda, MD 20817
   • A beautiful 90-minute tape of talks by Mother Teresa during her October 1975 visit to Mother Seton's Shrine, Baltimore and Washington, D.C., with background music by the Capuchin College Choir. $3.00.
   • A talk by Mother Teresa given in Washington, D.C. $2.50.

To obtain the two following tapes of Mother Teresa at the Eucharistic Congress in 1976, send $4.00 for each tape to: Congress Cassettes, P.O. Box 617, Ann Arbor, MI 48107.
   • A talk by Mother Teresa and Archbishop Helder Camara of Brazil. Number E.C. 302.
   • A talk by Mother Teresa, Dorothy Day, and Rosemary Goldie. Number E.C. 702.